HOW TO

Get Him Back

FROM THE

Other Woman

HOW TO

Get Him Back

FROM THE

Other Woman

IF YOU STILL WANT HIM

DIANE BARONI

·

BETTY KELLY

St. Martin's Press · New York

Design by Judith A. Stagnitto

0-312-08210-X

For Danielle, Elizabeth,
James, and Michael,
and for Helen Gurley Brown,
whose wit and wisdom
are a continuous inspiration.

There are two things to aim at
in life: first, to get what you want;
and, after that, to enjoy it.

—Logan Pearsall Smith,
Afterthought

CONTENTS

CHAPTER 1

So Now You Know: Where Do You Go From Here?

Fact: At least 70 percent of American husbands have had a sexual relationship outside of marriage. (Some studies put the figure as high as 90 percent.)

Fact: 75 to 85 percent of these men do not leave their wives permanently.

Fact: Of those men who do divorce, only 15 percent actually go on to marry the "other" woman.

Fact: 80 percent of the divorced men say they would remarry their wives if given the chance.

So now you know, and chances are you're shattered. Finding out that a husband or lover is having an affair is one of the most devastating discoveries a woman can make. And sadly, as you can see, countless numbers of women are making this discovery all the time. But however anguished, enraged, and confused you're feeling right now, try to take some comfort in edge that, if you want your man back, the odds are our favor. Remember that all-important fact: 75 to 85 all men who've had affairs end up staying with their wives, even if they've moved out for a while.

What we plan to do here is threefold. First, we're going to help you understand that the rage and disorientation you're feeling are perfectly normal, and we're going to give you clear and specific advice on how to cope with these feelings. Second, we're going to show you how to figure out whether or not you truly want this man back. And third, assuming the answer is yes, we're going to tell you exactly what to do to get him back—at least how to maximize the chances, which are already so heavily in your favor.

On the issue of a husband actually leaving his wife for the other woman, as in gambling, "the odds always seem to be with the house," says author Marion Zola, in *All the Good Ones Are Married*. But, you're probably wondering, if the chances of his coming back are so good, why bother to do anything at all? Well, there are several reasons. First, it's almost impossible to do nothing. You're so filled with rage and pain, your body knows instinctively that you need to do something—to move, to act. Passively waiting around for fate to take its course, even assuming you could, is bad for you; it makes you feel helpless, diminished, victimized. Also, the hands-off method requires such superhuman effort that, after a few weeks of doing nothing, a woman will tend to start ranting, accusing, threatening, using the children as pawns—all the tactics we strongly advise against. And finally, you don't just want your man back in body; you want him back on an entirely new basis of intimacy and trust. If you take no action, even if he does come back, those same old problems will be lurking around. Following our guidelines, on the other hand— doing what over a hundred women have told us worked for them—will help you win back not only his love but his trust and respect as well. Having a well-thought-out plan is your very best weapon, and we're going to show you how to custom-craft one for your particular situation.

Right now, though, it may be hard for you to think about the future because you are stunned. No matter how much you've

read about adultery being on the rise, you tho
tionship was different. You were convinced the
something special. You never dreamed he'd chea
there have been some rocky times, you trusted h.
You loved him, and you probably still do. You felt
entwined with him physically, emotionally, economi   ...y,
you just cannot believe that he would do this to you.

Well, stop right there. He hasn't done this *to you:* he's simply
done it. What's going on here has to do with his fragile ego—
not you. One thing you must constantly keep in mind if you are
going to save your relationship is that *you are not responsible for
his actions*—HE IS. What has happened is not your fault. Yes,
maybe he wasn't getting everything he needed from you, but
then you probably weren't getting everything you needed from
him, either. The important thing is not to blame yourself. You
are a separate, worthwhile, lovable person, and if you keep reminding yourself of this, your chances of getting him back, which,
as we've said, are already good, will increase dramatically.

But the problem is, right now you don't feel all that lovable.
Since so much of who you are, or who you think you are, is tied
up in your relationship with this man, your very identity has been
shaken so profoundly you may well believe you aren't going to
survive. Some of the women we talked to developed chronic
backaches, headaches, or dizziness; others were besieged with
phobias that ran the gamut from fear of the dark to fear of leaving
the house; some would sleep for twenty-four hours at a time
while others could hardly sleep at all. To a woman, they said
they could not control their crying. Something as minor as a
broken fingernail or being unable to find a parking space was
enough to set them off.

While these and other signs of depression are certainly unpleasant, it's helpful to know experts believe they're not only
normal but actually healthy. In her book *Crazy Time,* Abigail
Trafford quoted New York psychiatrist Frederic F. Flach as saying,
"A depressive response to a powerful stress is often ↄ sign of
normality, not weakness. A resilient patient not onl'
recovers but also grows from the experience. In fact

use self-denial, alcohol, or some other means to dodge *appropriate depression* are usually only postponing it. What finally arrives may be a profound and chronic depression."

And how could you not be depressed when everything about you has been undermined—your self-esteem, sense of security, desirability? Rejection is devastating, no matter how strong a woman you are; so is the idea that a relationship that has been such a central part of your life may be ending. California marriage and family counselor Daphne Rose Kingma, in *Coming Apart,* even goes so far as to say "next to the death of a loved one the ending of a relationship is the single most emotionally painful experience that any of us ever goes through." It's agonizing enough to feel that the person you love may no longer love you, but it's almost unbearable to be faced with the idea that he loves someone else. So it's hardly any wonder that for most women, suddenly, nothing matters—not career, not friends, not family; this man alone gave meaning to your existence—at least that's how you may feel right now. He was so smart, so sexy, so stable (or so you thought)—where will you ever find anyone else who measures up to such perfection? Without him, you feel worthless, helpless, paralyzed by panic.

"I'd always thought of myself as a pretty strong woman," says Margaret, a forty-five-year-old high school math teacher in Dearborn, Michigan. "But when Harold told me he was leaving home to move in with a woman he'd met at his office, I just collapsed. I simply could not believe it. All those childhood insecurities I thought I'd whipped came flooding back, and there were days when I couldn't even get out of bed. Thank God, it was spring vacation and the kids were visiting my parents in Florida. I was supposed to go to work for a series of conferences, but I called the school, lied and told them I had walking pneumonia, and then simply hid myself away. I hardly ate anything, and after about a week and a half, I was so thin and drawn I couldn't bear to look at myself in the mirror. I watched soaps all day and cried for hours at a time. Whenever I did have to go out to get some necessity or other, I was so paranoid I thought everybody was staring at me, thinking 'poor, pathetic thing; no wonder her husband dumped her.' It was really disturbed behavior, and I knew it, but I felt so numb I couldn't do anything about it. Finally, a neighbor talked me into going to see her therapist, and he was wonderful. He told me I was in shock, reassured me that it was a pretty normal reaction to such a crisis, and said the first thing I had to do was start eating. Then we'd get to less immediate matters . . . like whether or not my husband was the sort of man who was worth having back.

"It's interesting—even when I was at my very worst, there was this little voice somewhere deep inside me that kept saying, 'it's okay; you will pull through this; and you might even be surprised at what you're going to learn about yourself.' The voice was right. I did, and I am. What's more, I doubt anything could ever make me feel that shaky again. In the end, I decided that I didn't really want him back. And all the things I had learned about myself—that I could cope, that I was a survivor—helped me to make that decision."

Like Margaret, we all have that little voice, the one that says, "Well, this is a pretty rough one, but you're going to be fine." And it's more important now than ever in your life to listen to it. To help you hear it clearly, it might be useful to know about the emotional stages you'll probably pass through. We call them the six stages of healing, but whatever you want to call them, most people, when reacting to the shock of loss, or anticipated loss, go through these stages.

"Just as there is a set of clearly identified feelings that mark the grief-for-dying process, so there is also a series of clearly identifiable stages of feeling that people go through as they process the ending of a relationship," says Daphne Rose Kingma. She goes on to say, "any one of these feeling stages may be repeated one, or even many times." The threat of having a relationship end "creates a wound which must be healed and it follows that in order to complete the process of healing we may go through a given feeling or set of feelings numerous times. Healing doesn't happen overnight."

The reason it's important to know about these emotional stages, Kingma says, "is to give you an opportunity to validate the emotional experience you are having right now, to give you a sense of what is likely to come after what you are experiencing now, to let you know that the feelings you are having are appropriate, and to tell you that along with a multitude of others who have already gone through the process of parting, you too, will survive."

Kingma is one of the many experts who agree that certain stages exist. What the experts don't agree on is exactly what these stages are. We feel the following six capture the essence of the healing process as described by mental health professionals. Remember, you may not experience these stages in exactly the order we've listed them here, but chances are, as you try to work through what's happened, you'll have a brush with each of them.

THE SIX STAGES OF HEALING

DENIAL: STAGE ONE

This can't be true. It isn't really happening. I know I'll wake up in the morning and it will all have been a bad dream. Maybe he's just testing to see how much I care. Or maybe it's some sort of a sick joke. He's always had such a weird sense of humor.

Denial is invariably the first response to the news that your husband or lover has found someone else. Experts say it's the mind's way of protecting us from shock. The information you've received is so disorienting, disruptive, and unexpected you simply don't know how to process it. So you don't—at least not at first. On the one hand, you know it's true, but since what you've just found out is profoundly threatening, you're unable to deal with it. So you try to go on as if nothing had happened, telling yourself there must be some dreadful misunderstanding.

One woman we talked with said that on the same day she

learned her husband was having an affair, she prepared all his favorite foods, and served him a sumptuous candlelit dinner. Another woman went out and bought her husband a new suit. "He hadn't had a new one for two years and we were planning to do a lot of entertaining that summer," was her rationale. Still another woman called up a real estate agent and put in a bid on an expensive house she and her husband had looked at a month before. She did this exactly forty-five minutes after he told her he wanted to move in with his girlfriend.

It is during the denial stage, too, that women are most apt to have severe physical reactions, such as migraines or back pain. Some develop irrational fears for the first time in their lives, go on wild spending sprees, or become obsessive about little things they hardly noticed before. Almost everyone feels out of control during this phase, and that's normal. After all, you're charting new emotional territory here. You are not used to having such powerful feelings, and it is only natural to fear they'll overwhelm you. (They won't, but it's pretty hard to convince yourself of that right now.)

PANIC: STAGE TWO

I can't go on. Everything scares me. I'm afraid to turn off the lights at night. I can't concentrate on anything. I never want to get out of bed again.

This is the phase in which anxiety reactions can really begin to take over. You're not denying what's happened so much anymore, and the reality that your relationship is being threatened terrifies you. "How am I ever going to manage without him?" you wonder. "Who's going to mow the lawn and take out the Christmas tree? Who's going to pay the bills, play baseball with the kids? I just can't *do* all this alone," you think; "I've become so dependent on him."

Panic and anxiety reactions come in many forms. One woman was seized with terror every time she heard the smallest noise in the apartment—even called the police on several occasions. Another became agoraphobic and had to force herself to walk the two blocks to the supermarket. A third became panicked every time she had to enter an elevator . . . and this was no small problem, since she lived in New York City.

After a while, in each case the intensity of these reactions began to subside, but while at their worst they were profoundly unsettling. "I secretly thought I had lost my mind," the third woman told us. " 'So this is how it happens,' I thought. 'One day, you wake up and you're just crazy, off the wall.' And the worst of it is, you're terrified that you won't be able to keep the secret for very long."

Of course you're *not* off the wall, though it may feel that way at times. You're shocked, stressed, quite naturally frightened, but as with denial, these anxiety reactions are perfectly normal. Not having any feelings would actually be a real cause for concern. So grit your teeth and keep telling yourself you *will* survive. This too shall pass, and life *will* get better, just as it has for millions of other women.

GRIEF: STAGE THREE

> *I can't stop crying. Everything reminds me of him. He was my whole world; no one could ever replace him. That world is gray now—no colors anywhere. Nothing matters. I can barely eat—even key lime pie loaded with whipped cream (my favorite) doesn't tempt me. He was so precious, tender, loving, all-around wonderful, I don't know if I can go on without him.*

This passage, however anguishing, is vital because it allows you to begin to say goodbye to what was destructive in your relationship and start shaping a new and stronger identity for yourself. Of course he could be precious, tender, and loving, but those aren't the qualities he's been sharing with you lately, right? And yes, there are some great things about this man—that's why you chose him. But there were also some things that weren't so great, and it's important to take a look at them, too. Any loss is painful, and requires a period of mourning, but remember that at least some of what you've lost was destructive to you . . . and should be easy to let go of.

GUILT: STAGE FOUR

It's all my fault. If I'd been nicer, smarter, funnier, prettier, thinner (like she is), none of this would have happened. Why did I get so furious when he wanted his mom to move in with us, or when he wouldn't clean out the garage? If I'd only been a better wife, if only I hadn't gone back to work, we'd still be together.

This is the dangerous period when you start to examine everything about yourself, and hate it. You're too old, too fat, too mean, you tell yourself. Sure, you finished college in only three years, you've got two happy, healthy kids, and your rise at the office has been meteoric, but none of this seems to matter now. You loathe yourself; you feel powerless to do anything about what's going on. You're also awash in self-pity, and there may be times when you even toy with the idea of ending it all.

This stage can last anywhere from a day or two to weeks, even months, and the reason it's so dangerous is that if left unchecked, it can turn into a full-fledged depression, which might require professional help to undo. So again, remember you're a lovable, valuable human being, and that what he did has nothing to do with you. True, there were problems in the relationship, but there are problems in every relationship and many men confront and try to work them out with the women they love. Your man didn't; right now he's wrestling with his own demons, his own neuroses, and they have very little to do with you. You can't control his behavior, but you *can* take charge of yours. Somewhere, deep inside, you know it's irrational to blame yourself for

ir, so listen to that sound advice and take it to heart. Tell
f that *somebody* has to stay sane around here.

ANGER: STAGE FIVE

It's all his fault. He's a coward and a wimp and I hate him. How could he do this to me after I worked nights to help put him through law school? He was always cold, cruel, insensitive and I'll never forgive him.

Now, you're in the flip side of the guilt phase. You're no longer turning fury inward and becoming depressed; you're venting your emotions all over the place, and the mere mention of his name sends you into a rage. As in all the other phases we've described, this rage is a perfectly normal part of the healing process—but one word of caution. Some women get stuck at this point, and waste years hating him—and the whole male population—rather than getting on with their lives.

Sally is a pretty, thirty-four-year-old real estate agent who, three years after her husband left her for another woman, until recently could talk of almost nothing else. "Do you know what the bastard did this time? He went with *her* to the Caribbean and wouldn't even give me money to take the kids out west for a week. Not only that, I called him one night at eleven to talk about Mary's homework and he said it was too late to have phoned him. He's so rude and selfish, I just can't stand him. He was never much of a husband anyway."

Allowing yourself to become stuck in the bitterness-and-anger phase can be almost as destructive as getting locked in self-blame. Wild mood swings and constant vacillations between rage and depression are to be expected, but if you find yourself at an impasse, do something about it. Sally didn't see how tedious her ranting about her ex-husband was becoming, or that it was preventing her from opening up to life. Only when she forced herself to stop raving and start assessing that relationship—which she soon realized had only made her unhappy—was she able to move ahead. It's important to remember that unrelieved bitterness ultimately hurts the person indulging in it more than the person it's directed at.

ACCEPTANCE: STAGE SIX

Okay, he did what he did, and that's that. I certainly don't like what he did, but I understand some of the reasons for it. I know his affair wasn't my fault, and although I once thought I'd never be able to forgive him, finally, I have. And in some ways, I think we're now going to have an even better relationship than before. We're much more honest with each other, more sensitive. And after going through all we did, we certainly know each other better. I can't say I'm glad it happened, but his leaving forced us to look at some pretty powerful stuff we'd been avoiding.

This is the phase when you're finally able to accept what has happened, reestablish your equanimity, and get on with the business of living your life. You can reach it long before the outcome of your relationship is resolved, and the sooner you get there, the better—for you. Once you're back on solid ground, you will be able to evaluate in a much more clear headed way whether or not you even want this man to play such a major role in your life again. And if indeed you do, you'll be far better equipped to write the script.

"Finally, I was able to say to myself 'It's true; Rob really is involved with another woman,' " says a forty-three-year-old executive assistant. "Only then could I take a look at some of the reasons it happened. Once I did, Rob and I were able to talk about some painful truths we'd been avoiding for years. He decided he wanted to try again, to give it his best this time, and so far, we're getting along better than we ever have before. In some ways, it seems like a whole new relationship. I feel a lot more positive about myself, and I think that makes a big difference. We're also more careful of each other's feelings; we listen better. I wish Rob hadn't had the affair, of course, but ironically, I think it may have saved our marriage."

As we've said, working through these phases can take weeks, months, and in some cases even longer, so try not to get discouraged. You may think you're finished with the guilt phase and then, surprise, it resurfaces just when you least expect it. But don't worry—*all* these phases have a sneaky way of popping up again and again until you are able to resolve the self-doubt, blame, anger—until you have truly come to grips with what has happened.

In the meantime, though, there are four absolute taboos we want to tell you about. These are things you'll want to do more than anything, but you really must *force* yourself not to give in to them.

ABSOLUTE DO-NOTS

1. DO NOT ISOLATE YOURSELF

We know it's not easy to keep on going to work and taking your turn at the carpool after gymnastics class when you're in such pain, but every women we talked to said that in her experience, the last thing she wanted to do was change her routine. "I think my volunteer work at the library and the routine that went along with it saved me," says Sara, a sixty-four-year-old Connecticut woman whose husband marched out one day after a forty-four-year marriage. "I told my friends about Ron and his new 'girlfriend,' of course, and they were wonderful, but what really kept me going was doing what I had always done. I got up at the same time, got dressed, had coffee in the same hand-painted mug from Italy, and then went off to the library, where I felt secure, surrounded by people who knew me. It was the day-to-dayness of having some friendly place to go that kept me sane—well, not completely sane, but balanced enough to get through the worst of the shock."

2. DO NOT STOP EATING

As we've seen, not eating is one of the classic symptoms of shock depression. Sometimes women in such a state become so estranged from their basic needs, or so subconsciously self-destructive, they simply can't face even the sight of food. Clever diet technique you may be thinking, but that's far from the case. Now, when there's so much stress, so much disorientation in your life, you need nourishment more than ever—and that means physical as well as emotional.

Some women have the opposite response, and begin to eat compulsively when they're in shock. Obviously this isn't a good idea, either. All your shaky self-esteem needs right now is a body that's ten pounds overweight—so make a big effort to avoid using food for comfort purposes. Whatever your eating problem during this tension-filled period, you should concentrate on healthy, well-balanced, regular meals. Just make yourself do it; the old love-your-body stuff really works, and watching your diet is one concrete way to show that you do. Eating properly may seem trivial compared to what else is going on, but it's not. In fact, it's just about the most important short-run action you can take.

3. DO NOT DRINK TOO MUCH

We know the temptation is great. It seems so relaxing just to have a couple of extra cocktails, or a bottle of wine, but the fact is, alcohol is a depressant and is only going to make you feel worse—much worse. If you've always enjoyed a drink or two before dinner, this is certainly no time to give the ritual up, but promise yourself you'll take care to stop there. Your health is vital right now, and the last thing you want to do is threaten it with alcohol overload. It may sound silly at first, but when you start to crave just one more little vodka on the rocks, why not try something as simple as jumping rope instead? Exercise, even the most modest type—walking up and down the stairs a few times, doing kneebends, or, yes, jumping in place—can do wonders to lift depression and restore your sense of well-being.

4. DO NOT OBSESS ABOUT *HER*

One of the most natural—and destructive—things you can do when you find out the man you love and trust has been unfaithful is to become obsessed with the other woman. It not only diminishes your already wobbly self-image, it saps precious vitality so that you can't get on with the task at hand—pulling yourself together, or at least appearing to, so you can focus on what to do next.

"I wanted to kill her," Barbara, a forty-two-year-old cosmetics executive, says, recalling the day she learned that her husband of eleven years was having an affair with a twenty-two-year-old artist. "I'm not kidding—I really tried to think up some way to put a bomb in her mailbox, or rat poison in her sugar bowl, without getting caught, but I just couldn't come up with anything that seemed doable and foolproof.

"Then, after that phase passed, I wanted to *be* her. I pictured some gorgeous *Playboy* centerfold who looked like Kim Bassinger, and was the hottest young talent to hit the art scene since Georgia O'Keeffe. I kept staring into the mirror and imagining her taut, thin thighs, her concave tummy, and comparing them to mine. *I just couldn't get her out of my mind.* I spent hours lurking around her apartment house, hoping to spot her, or them. I even went to the gallery where her paintings had recently been exhibited, and pretended to be an interested patron. Needless to say, I was thrilled when I learned that none of her paintings had been sold during the show. The only tense moment came when the owner of the gallery asked for my name and address for their mailing list. But I just made up an address and gave the name of an old friend from high school. Looking back, I realized I was trying to blame the other woman and myself for what had happened, rather than confront the fact that it was my husband who was actually causing all the pain."

Of course you're curious, and furious, and there will be times when you can't help imagining that she's a paragon of strength and sensuality (despite what people who know better have told you) but you really must fight that impulse. She is *not* better than you, just different. It is *not* her fault that he's strayed (although she certainly may have been a willing participant), any more than it is your fault. He is a grown-up. He made the decision to do what he's done, so try not to waste valuable time and energy on her. You are the one who matters now, and you are the one you must care about and concentrate on. So, hard as it may be, forget about her. If it's any comfort at all, she's got her own problems.

By all accounts, the other woman is going through hell, too. "For all the suicide threats of wives who are left, I heard about more attempts and successes on the part of the other woman," says author Marion Zola. Why is she so depressed? Because she has an unerring gut instinct that in the end he will not leave you for her. And (remember those statistics), in most cases, he won't.

Suppose, for example, that even though the affair is now out in the open, he's still living at home. Where do they meet for all this high-flying passion? At her apartment? What if she has roommates or lives in a one-room studio furnished in early orange crate (which makes it a touch difficult to present a sexy, swinging single girl image)? Or suppose they connect in a hotel (pretty tacky, no?) and she has to walk through the lobby feeling that *everybody* knows (certainly, the smirking desk clerk knows). Then, too, however seductive her skimpy black lace panties, however soaring the sex, there will always be that anguishing moment when he fumbles for his watch on the bedside table and says something like, "Honey, I'd love to stay; you know I would. Someday, I promise, someday *soon,* we'll be together for good.

It's just that tonight, we're having people for dinner—my boss and his wife, actually—and. . . ." He's been making such getaway excuses for months. He dresses hurriedly, and leaves, and there the girlfriend is, alone in a hotel room, in the dark, with only the faint scent of his Brut on the pillow for company. *Don't you think she worries about all this?*

Or say he has moved out, and is either living with her or in an apartment of his own. If he's already made that grand gesture, why, she wonders, won't he commit—get a divorce and marry her? Why does he keep going *home* (to see the kids, check on the pipes, find "that sweater Di knitted for me; the one I can't live without)?" *What is he waiting for?* It's enough to drive a girl crazy. (It is driving the girl crazy.) So, you don't have to feel sorry for the woman, but you shouldn't obsess about the fabulous time she's having. Her position is much more tenuous than yours.

Consider, too, that even now, in the first flush of new "love," your man probably isn't feeling so wonderful, either. The typical errant husband or lover is torn by guilt, anxiety, indecisiveness. Deep down, he's terrified of change, extremely concerned about his position in the community, his image of himself as a decent, responsible person. He's as worried about money as you are—perhaps more so. He loves the kids, and what is more important, there's a very good chance he still loves you, truly wants to come home on some level (even if, at present, he isn't aware of that fact). Given all this, if you love the man, is there any valid reason not to start trying to get him back with everything you've got?

It's astounding how many strong, sensible women will fight for a well-deserved promotion, fight to be sure their children get a good education, fight to get proper care for aging parents—yet when it comes to fighting for the man they love, they back off. The feeling is either fury (if he doesn't want me, the hell with him; let him go) or a passivity that is rather suspect (I can't force him to stay with me if he doesn't want to). Whatever the extreme, it's a fact that, initially, most women are uncomfortable with the idea of trying to get a man back. "Degrading." "Hopeless." "Weak." These are the words you most often hear used when they describe their feelings.

Partly, those reactions are due to the relentless hype we've been exposed to for the past twenty or so years. Women are supposed to be proud, totally self-sufficient creatures with principles—one wrong move on a man's part and it's off to the divorce lawyer's. Forget the devastating effects on children. Forget a sudden, often frighteningly lowered standard of living. (In a widely quoted report by sociologist Lenore Weitzman of Harvard University, a woman's standard of living was said to drop 73 percent after divorce. This statistic was refuted by other studies, which gave a 33 percent decline in the first two years, but an increase by five years after the split. Still, 33 percent over twenty-four months isn't exactly fun and games, either.) Forget that five out of six divorced women receive no alimony at all—you're supposed to get out there and be a Contemporary Woman—miserable, maybe, but at least you've taken no nonsense from the male sex.

Similarly, when we see women like Elizabeth Taylor or Joan Collins splitting from men who fooled around or who didn't measure up in other ways, we tend to ignore the millions of dollars, widespread support systems, and glittery social opportunities available to such celebrities. Suddenly, *we* are on the witness stand, lights and cameras on us, courageously tossing an errant husband or lover out of our lives for good. After our moment in the sun is over, however, few of us have the wherewithal to zoom to Paris on the Concorde or repair to Bali for a month to help us through the painful aftermath.

Friends, both male and female, aren't much help, either. They tend to be incredibly supportive of a woman's decision to let a man go (and of a man's desire to leave, even if his reason is as lightweight as "needing space"), but not of her fight to save the relationship. They figuratively avert their heads, as if embarrassed that anyone would admit, in these supposedly freewheeling days, that a relationship is worth saving. Relationships seem to have become as expendable as appliances on the blink. The refrigerator's making a funny knocking sound? Out with it! The VCR's a little fuzzy? Buy a new one! Actually *fixing* things, in a culture crammed with disposables, seems as dated a concept as the maxi-skirt. If it isn't in perfect working order, toss it.

Yet another reason we shy away from fighting to win back a

man who's involved with another woman is that the whole process seems so hopeless. Adultery is definitely on the upswing, and indeed, "most men do." (Many women "do," too, of course—about 50 percent at last count—but we're not concerned with that here.) Isn't it a little naïve to try to pit yourself against a national—or even global—trend?

Strangely enough, accepting that adultery exists can be quite freeing. Once you set aside rosy romantic expectations and realize that, happily or not, infidelity is a part of life, you're better able to fight it. Disease, poverty, myriad forms of man's inhumanity to man are also a part of life, but to most people, it would be unthinkable simply to sit back and let the devastation take its course. The fact that cancer exists, for instance, does not mean the average sufferer will not go to almost any length to try to cure it; someone who has been injured in an automobile accident will fight to walk again through often agonizing physical therapy sessions. And the same should go for trying to save a relationship. Of course you would rather your man had not joined the growing number of husbands and lovers who stray, but he did. And now it's up to you to save the relationship, him, and yourself.

That is not to say that any woman should fight to stay in a union in which a man is abusive, or in which she is so unfulfilled and miserable she can barely function. We'll talk about how to decide whether you're better off without this man in the next chapter. Still, the ease with which so many women give up men they truly love and want to spend their lives with is worth thinking hard about.

Without question, it takes enormous courage to fight for a man at a time when your self-esteem is at an all-time low. You can't help feeling low when someone you love, and with whom you've been through so much, has, by virtue of having an affair, implied that you mean nothing to him. As California psychologist Diana Medved points out in *The Case Against Divorce:* "For you to say [to your man] 'Wait a minute, you're throwing away the best thing you've got, something precious and worth saving,' makes you feel like a hypocrite. How can you tell your partner how great you are when you don't believe it yourself? How can you summon up the *chutzpah* to sound self-assured and confident when you're reeling from a debilitating blow to your self-esteem? It's much easier to slump into helplessness and accept the situation as it's presented to you: He doesn't love you; it's his decision; you can't get into his head and change his mind."

Medved's right—passive acceptance is indeed far easier than facing the arduous task of trying to get your man back. But as she goes on to note, such behavior also gives him even more justification to leave. "She's just accepting what I tell her, so she must want me to leave," he can figure. Or, he can point to your behavior to prove your inferiority, as in: "I know she still loves me, but look at her—she's just whimpering around, depressed. Why should I want to stay with someone like that—someone with so little spunk and gumption that she won't even fight to keep me?" Either way, you look pathetic.

And pathetic is the last thing you want to seem. To begin with, it is disastrous for your self-image. It almost never wins a man back. And if by some fluke it should, remember that using pity to further your aims—whether it be in love, friendship, or work—*is* degrading. Not only that, the partner's return is almost always short-lived, and even if the relationship does last, it will never be one built on a foundation of mutual respect and devotion, but rather on fear (yours, of his leaving again) and a weary sense of responsibility (his). What invariably does win a man back— and on a valid basis—is quiet determination coupled with courage and an unshakable sense of self-worth. All the women we talked with possessed these qualities, if not at the point at which they learned about the affair, then soon afterward. Although their lives were crumbling around them, they forced themselves not to crumble—they found the right support systems, unearthed new strengths, never lost sight of their goals.

An affair, then, does not necessarily signal the end of a relationship; it is how you handle the affair that affects the outcome. As Dr. Frank Pittman, a psychiatrist and family therapist in Atlanta, Georgia, and author of *Private Lies: Infidelity and the Betrayal of Intimacy,* notes: "Certainly an affair is a crisis in a relationship. After any crisis, the relationship may become better and it may become worse. Some people divorce after an affair, some remain married and punitive and miserable, and others use the affair as a crisis from which to produce a more satisfactory marriage."

Admittedly, it's hard to think about having a more satisfactory relationship when you're churning with conflicting and painful emotions, but starting right now, there are three points you *must* remember:

1. *Put yourself first.* Ironically, the most important decision you can make right now has nothing to do with him: you must start focusing on your *own* life. You're the most important person in the world at this moment, and your self-worth does not depend on him, so try to avoid getting caught in a vortex of self-destructive feelings. You are not to blame for what he did; no person controls another's actions. Maybe you should have seen it coming (maybe you even did), but that's not the point. The point is that you are a valuable, lovable, worthwhile woman, and when the emotional storm calms down, you'll be better able to figure out the appropriate course of action to take.

2. *Do not fall apart in front of him, no matter what.* Even if you have visions of becoming a bag lady or of being reduced to putting ads in the personals ("desperate, lonely, unloved thirty-four-year-old nobody seeks male anybody; smokers, all religions okay; height and weight not considerations"), do not let him see your panic, ever. "The best observation of professionals and wives indicate that the vital thing is to avoid panic" in front of him, says Marion Zola. "A wife's highly emotional, vengeful behavior ends up being destructive to *her* rather than her husband."

3. *Create desire, not guilt.* Loading him with guilt may have some effect initially, but it's making him want you again that pays off in the long run. And to do that, you can't simply keep smiling understandingly (or crying constantly) and wait it out—you have to pique his interest; let him see you as a strong, sexy woman; remind him of what it was he loved about you in the first place. You have to, in other words, act—sensibly, positively,

and yes, a little craftily. You must set aside the inclination to fall into the role of victim, and start thinking war.

"You can admit defeat . . . or fight," says Medved. "You don't have to accept it when your partner tries to convince you that you have nothing in common or that the passion has died. And while it's true that ultimately you can't force someone to love or stay married to you, you can certainly make it difficult to leave, physically and emotionally. This sounds somehow unfair or devious, but it's really not at all—in fact, the purpose is to prevent disaster."

That disaster is the end of a relationship you feel is worth saving, and its attendant loss of love, support, security, friendship, comfort. But never forget that the loss is not just for you, but for him. If you can possibly find it in yourself to look at the situation altruistically, you'll see that, in effect, you are about to try to save your man from himself. Statistics show that it's more than likely he will not be happier if he leaves, and will deeply regret having left. You might try, as one woman did, to equate his current behavior, hurtful as it is, with his having a bad case of flu. Except in those rare cases when the illness turns into something more serious, it's relatively short term, and if taken care of, leaves no major lasting effects.

If you want to, you *can* get your man back—all the women we talked to did, and without losing their self-respect. They were often afraid. Sometimes ambivalent. And their pain cannot be denied. But in the end, strength, courage, humor, and, yes, even compassion, carried them through. We hope their stories, and the advice of psychiatrists, marriage counselors, and other experts will help you in your quest. Actually, we know they will.

One final word of encouragement: Researchers have found that in many cases, such affairs often fizzle out at the very moment they seem hottest. So remember, it's highly probable that he *will* be back, and in the meantime, patience and fortitude are the best short-term postures you can possibly take.

CHAPTER 2

Do You

Really Want

Him Back?

Here comes the hard part. As devastated as you feel right now—as disoriented, humiliated, and just plain mad—you must force yourself to stand back emotionally and take a cool, objective look at who this man really is, and whether or not he's good for you. No question—on the surface, at least—it would be easier for you two to stay together than to part. So much of your identity and sense of security are tied up with being part of a pair that the very thought of tampering with the status quo almost certainly has you terrified. And there's no point in pretending you're not going to wobble; facing a life change as major as ending a relationship is scary. But believe it or not, Daphne Kingma notes, "it also provides an extraordinary opportunity for growth."

Oh, great—growth, you say to yourself. Why risk heartache, personal hell, petty fights about who gets the parakeet and Wyeth lithograph for the questionable joys of growth when you might be able to patch things up and go on as if nothing had ever happened? Well, first of all, because it's impossible to go on as if nothing ever happened. Something *has* happened. Second, if this man is unwilling or unable to give you what you need, you'll never be happy with him, anyway—and now's the time to face that unpleasant fact, not five or fifteen years down the line.

Try looking at it this way. Whether or not you finally decide you want him back, whether or not you get him back, you're in this situation anyway. Not a situation of your own making, but still, you're in it. Why, then, wouldn't it be a good idea to at least consider using this tough but potentially productive period to test your limits? You have everything to gain and nothing to lose. "I have watched as time and again," says Kingma, "after anguishing crises in self-esteem, my clients emerged from their shattered relationships with enhanced self-images, redefined careers, recaptured creativity, pared-down, toned-up bodies, bad habits lost, new habits gained—in short, transformed identities."

So let's forget about him for a minute, and take a hard look at you. Try to set aside all those self-defeating thoughts that keep circling around and around in your head: *Why didn't I keep at those thigh-paring exercises . . . if only I hadn't gotten so mad that night he brought the entire bowling team back for dinner . . . Maybe I should have had my breasts done.* The simple truth is that you are not responsible for what he's done—he is. You *cannot* control his behavior; you can only control your own—even though it probably doesn't feel that way right now. Perhaps the reason you contributed your fair share to the relationship's problems (you were angry, frustrated a lot, and showed it) is that you simply weren't getting enough of what you needed. So stop tearing yourself apart! Instead, tell yourself over and over (you don't have to actually believe it yet) that you're a perfectly okay woman who deserves to be loved, have fun, be happy. Make it your own personal mantra. Then ask the private part of you that always tells the truth (everybody has one, so if it's not instantly available owing to lack of practice, keep searching) exactly what you were missing. Did you feel cared for, pampered, appreciated? Was the alliance a nurturing one in which you were encouraged to develop and express your real self? Does this man have the qualities you need to feel both secure and stimulated in life, and is he willing to share them with you? Was he physically available? And what is more important, was he emotionally available? Do you feel that with work and cooperation on his part you'll be able to trust him again, or has he consistently given you cause for concern—by flirting obsessively with everyone from waitresses to your friends? These are only a few of the questions you should ask yourself—and if you've answered no to most of them, you're probably already getting the feeling that maybe he's not the man for you.

More questions—and answer as truthfully as you can, even if it hurts. Remember, this isn't a contest; nobody's keeping score. You're not out to dissect the man, or see only what he's lacking; but you do have to face the possibility that he's simply incapable of being the sort of life companion you're after. Ready to get honest? Here we go:

- Did he listen to you, weigh what you had to say?
- Did he ask how you felt, what you wanted?
- Was he affectionate?
- Did you laugh, have fun together?
- Was he proud of your accomplishments?
- Did he delight in introducing you to his friends?
- Was he eager to make you happy in bed?
- Did he make you feel like the most fabulous lover on earth, or at least like a very desirable woman?
- This incident aside, did he avoid making you jealous of other women?
- Was he truthful?
- Did he usually do what he said he was going to do?
- Was he responsible financially?
- Were you compatible in terms of interests?
- Did it make him happy to make you happy?
- Did you trust him?

- Did you respect him?
- Were you proud of him?
- Was he willing to admit mistakes?
- Did he share thoughts and feelings without constant p...
  ding?
- Was he tender?
- Did you have the same values?
- Does he still turn you on?
- Did he appreciate you?
- Did you feel secure with him?
- Was he your best friend?
- If you'd known then what you know now about him, would you still marry or live with him?

Now for the really tough questions:

- Were you sometimes afraid of him?
- Did he criticize you too much?
- Did he use drugs?
- Was he a compulsive gambler?
- Did he ever get violent, hit you and/or the kids?
- Was he angry a lot?
- Did you sometimes wonder if he had real mental problems?
- Did he ever force you to have sex?
- Did he ever withhold sex for long periods of time?
- Was he into kinky sex play that made you feel uncomfortable, even frightened you?
- Was he chronically unfaithful?

Before we deal with less black-and-white areas, if the answer to any of this last batch of questions is yes, then your man's affair may well be just the catalyst you need to help you separate your fantasy of him from the reality of *who he actually is.* Violence, whether verbal or physical, is simply unacceptable. And a man bent on self-destruction through drugs, drinking, gambling, or other compulsive behavior is only going to drag you down with him. (If he agrees to get professional help, that could be another story, but you'll still want to see what the outcome is before making a final decision.)

Any man who uses philandering as a way to hurt you is also extremely suspect. "I once had a patient who left a used condom in his wife's car," says New York psychoanalyst Jeanne Safer. "It's pretty obvious he wanted her to find out about his affair. You wouldn't believe what some men do—leave love letters around, charge motel rooms to MasterCard . . . in one case I was supervising, the woman's husband had an affair with her sister. In such cases, the whole purpose is obviously to hurt the wife or girlfriend. It's always a bad sign if your man has an affair with a relative or friend of yours, or in any situation that would humiliate you publicly, because it means there's a tremendous amount of aggression and rage being acted out on his part. You have to assess how much hostility was involved in the act; his having an affair with your sister is very different from his going to a convention, say, and having a fling."

If your man's behavior has continuously hurt you, chances are you're in a codependent relationship. While the term *codependency* was originally coined to explain the overly dependent relationships between alcoholics and the people who most closely share their lives, its meaning has been expanded to encompass many forms of destructive behavior. One expert on the subject, Emily Marlin, past president of the New York Association for Marriage and Family Therapy, notes that one of her patients described being a codependent as "chasing after someone else's rainbow."

"Codependents," Marlin explains in *Relationships in Recovery,* "completely neglect themselves and the satisfaction of their own wants, needs, and desires. As they see themselves, they have only one value and purpose: To service another person's wants and needs. That other person becomes the sole raison d'être of a codependent's life. And as this self-negation gathers momentum, a codependent's identity becomes buried in the other person."

So it isn't simply that your man is hooked on alcohol or drugs, or is physically or psychologically abusive; it's that you have become hooked on his behavior, because dealing with and accepting that behavior is where you feel your value and purpose lie.

Another expert, Denver psychotherapist Carolyn Bushong, puts it this way in *Loving Him Without Losing You:* "Any time we accept [such behavior], we are accepting someone else's opinion about us without challenging it, for fear of losing their approval. This in turn keeps our self-esteem low, helps the abuser continue his behavior and keeps us addicted to their love." Bushong goes on to say she feels that "it is the desperate craving for love that is at the core of *all* addiction; it's the denial of the need to be loved and approved of that causes such incredible pain that we want to drink or use drugs to hide from life . . . or put up with abusive behavior from a man."

What sort of woman is most prone to codependency? If you didn't get the love and attention you needed when you were growing up, were abused or abandoned, or lived in a family where affection and approval were rare, you're a prime candidate.

"The tendency of individual codependents to undervalue themselves usually becomes established long before adulthood," says Marlin. "Like the majority of alcoholics, most codependents grew up in addictive households. Alcoholic and codependent parents instill in their children values of responsibility, loyalty, selflessness, taking care of others, and helpfulness. But in the chaos of addictive families, these selfless virtues become overvalued. During their formative years, codependents learn to take these positive, helping traits to self-destructive extremes; responsible becomes hyper-responsible, loyalty becomes blind devotion, and selflessness become self-negation. Because they have been taught to put other people's needs before their own, codependents become martyrs and victims in their own lives."

"It always seemed to me that I was put on earth to take care of others—specifically, my mother," says Susanna, a thirty-two-year-old researcher for a San Francisco publishing firm.

> From the time I was a very little girl, I sensed that, to win my father's approval, I had to watch over her. My mother was a dear, beautiful but extremely childlike woman who was also an alcoholic—not a falling-down drunk, but an alcoholic just the same. As soon as my father left for work in the morning, she started sipping bourbon, and she kept

on sipping throughout the day. I can still close my eyes and smell that sweet, heavy smell. She was totally unequipped to have a child herself, and in fact, hadn't wanted one—it was my father who had insisted. That put still another burden on me. I had to prove that he'd been right to want me.

Mother's needs always came first. I'd hurry back from school so that I could monitor her drinking, try to sober her up a little before my father got home. Even when I was in my teens, those normal years for rebellion, it never occurred to me that my feelings or needs meant anything, that I deserved to have a life of my own. I even gave up going to a party, one of the few parties I'd ever been invited to, because that night she kept crying and begging me not to leave her alone—my father was off on a business trip. Only once, when I was helping her get dressed for dinner, and she was very high, going on and on about how, if only she hadn't married my father, if only she hadn't had a child, she could have been a famous actress, did the glimmer of a thought hit me: *This is all wrong. I should be telling her my problems.* I should be talking about what *I* want to be. I should be talking about boys, and how much I liked this one boy in my grade, but I didn't know whether or not he liked me. I should be talking about how lonely I felt sometimes, and how scared. But of course, I didn't say anything. I just fastened her dress and kept on brushing her hair.

When I married Adam, I now see that I simply carried on the same pattern. Oh, he wasn't an alcoholic, but he was incredibly demanding. He put me down all the time; nothing I could do was right. But still, I kept trying. All I thought about was his needs, what he wanted. It got so bad that consciously, at least, I had no feelings or thoughts of my own. But at the same time, I was certain he couldn't function without me. I thought I could save him, turn him into the warm, loving man that, against all evidence, I believed him to be underneath.

It may seem strange to say this, but Adam's affair forced me to act. He was so blatant about it, so cruel. He'd throw his shirt down on the bed and yell at me because the laundry hadn't ironed it properly; what was he supposed to do, go meet his lover wearing a wrinkled shirt? He'd tell me how good in bed she was, compared to me. It was as if he was daring me to react. And finally, I did. I moved out, and asked my father to help me pay for therapy—it was the first time I'd ever asked him for anything in my entire life. And believe it or not, he did; he must have sensed how bad it was.

My therapist is a wonderful woman. I really trust her. We've gone over the past, and acknowledged it. But she constantly pushes me to put it behind me, make a life for myself. I can't say it's easy, but inch by inch, I'm getting there.

However painful your past, you really can, as Suzanna did, overcome its effects and become the whole, self-reliant, self-loving person you were always meant to be. Many women need the help of an understanding, supportive therapist to accomplish that end; others just dive in and will themselves to change because they've absolutely had it with neglecting their own needs. It doesn't much matter which route you take; the main thing is that you make a concentrated effort to start changing—now.

"To break emotional dependencies and become self-reliant, we must learn to stop caring whether others are pleased by our behavior, and learn to enjoy being alone," says Bushong. "We must forgive ourselves for not being as perfect as our parents and society—and we—wish we were." We also have to figure out what our feelings are, appreciate and express them—even when they aren't "nice." We have to take control of our lives and be willing to take a few risks. Now. As Bushong says, we should stop *talking* and start *doing,* forget about "muddling in and analyzing our problems, and instead take the action necessary to make our lives the way we want them to be. Then and only then will we truly have an identity that no man, parent or authority will ever take away from us."

Marlin agrees: "You will need to take the initiative if you really want to get what you want out of life. You can't just wait for the things you want to drop into your lap. If you want others to care for you, you will need to begin caring for yourself as much as you care for others. Similarly, if you want to win the respect of others, you need to begin by developing some self-respect. And you can start to have some fun simply by doing more frequently the things that give you pleasure. After years of self-denial, you deserve to get what you want. And though you can't *always* get what you want, you'll never get it if you don't try. So don't just wait for change to come to you; actively seek and promote change within and outside yourself."

As tough as it is, if it's becoming all too evident that involvement with this man can only bring you more grief, you have little choice but to move on—sad, yes, but at least clear-cut.

But what if the issue isn't so clear-cut? What if he doesn't drink a bottle of vodka a night, or abuse you or the children, but you still found yourself answering no to more than half the questions in the first group? Deciding whether or not you really want him back is then obviously more difficult. Do you arbitrarily pick a number—twenty out of twenty-six no's and he's history?

Not at all. What works for one woman isn't necessarily going to work for another. It depends on your priorities. Some women couldn't care less about "interesting" conversation—great sex, and a lot of it, is first on their list. Others are willing to pretty much forget about having the same values; having fun is what matters most. So (as everybody from us to the Bible keeps telling you), you have to know yourself to decide what you can live with and without.

You are what matters, not what the rest of the world thinks. Forget friends who say he doesn't appreciate you enough. Forget sadistic "experts" who insist that to be happy in bed, you have to have incendiary sex every night, and if he can't service you in this heady fashion, out with him! No man is going to possess all the good qualities outlined in the previous questions. If yours does, there's got to be something fishy about him—like those infamous Don Juans who con little old ladies out of their savings.

One simple way to help you figure out if the man in your life is right for you was conceived by New York clinical psychologist Judy Kuriansky. In *How to Love A Nice Guy,* she suggests you imagine yourselves alone together on a desert island—no movies, boutiques, or distractions of any kind—and consider the following:

"What do you talk about? How would you be together? How do you rely on each other? Does he listen to you? As you talk, do you speak about how you feel inside and what your dreams are? What do you like about being on the island? What feels good to you? What do you think about getting off the island— do you want to get off? Where do you want to go? Do you like being alone together? Does he? Do you feel good together?" "If you didn't like being on the island together," says Kuriansky, "you've got a pretty good indication that you have a relationship built on things that die, get lost or end."

What this test actually measures is the depth of your relationship. If you're beginning to suspect that it's been held together by only a thin layer of glue—you "needed" Calvin Kleins; he "needed" a good hostess for business dinners—rather than true intimacy, then, you've got to level with yourself about the difference between what you need and what you're getting . . . and whether or not this particular man can give it to you.

Another way to help you assess whether or not you really want him back, says psychoanalyst Jeanne Safer, is to make two lists, one headed *bad reasons* and the other *good reasons.* You may be surprised to learn what your true motivations are. Here's what one woman wrote:

WHY I WANT HIM BACK

Bad Reasons

- I'm afraid of being alone.
- No one will ever love me again.
- I'm embarrassed—I don't want people to think I can't keep a man.
- Even though he's not great, he's probably the best I can do.
- I don't want to go through the trauma of being a "single woman."
- I'm terrified of trying to find a new man.
- I like the social status he brings.
- I hate change.
- I need the security he offers.
- Without him I feel like nothing.
- Going through a divorce just doesn't seem worth the effort.
- All my friends are married or coupled—I don't want to be different.
- Even though we don't get along, we should stay together for the kids' sake.
- I'm too old to ever find another man.

Good Reasons

- We're similar in tastes and outlook.
- He's basically a warm, kind, sensitive person.
- Even now, I admire and respect him.
- We still laugh at the same things.
- He's my soul mate.
- We can talk openly to each other.
- He's always been supportive of me.
- We have the same goals.
- We're emotionally compatible.

- We have intellectual rapport.
- He's great in bed, satisfies me like no other man.
- No matter what, he's my best friend.
- I want to spend the rest of my life with him.

Let's tackle the bad reasons first so we can get them over with. It isn't hard to see why it's not such a terrific idea to stay with a man because you're afraid of being alone or because you don't want to be different from your friends. Here's someone who's betrayed and humiliated you, you're not even that crazy about him, and yet, because of your own insecurities, you're willing to stick it out. Of course, it's frightening to think about building a new life for yourself, but every woman we talked to who eventually decided to do just that wound up much happier and more productive than when trapped in an unfulfilling (or worse) relationship. And this was as true for the women in their forties, fifties, and sixties as for those in their thirties. Listen to Marisa, a forty-two-year-old public relations executive from Chicago as she talks about the summer she discovered her forty-five-year-old husband was having an affair with their French *au pair*:

> I can't believe how naïve I was. We'd been married for eleven years, our kids were five and eight, and during the summer, Fred—I'll call him—who had his own graphic design business, would often work out of our house in the country while I stayed in town and came up on weekends. We'd done this for several years, and I'd always been lucky with babysitters—or so I thought.
> It's a typical story, I guess. One Thursday in August, I decided to surprise everybody by coming up a day early. When I arrived that night at about ten, the kids were asleep, and there he was in my bed with her—that gorgeous little nineteen-year-old *au pair*. I just about died. Fred swore it had never happened before, that they'd had too much to drink, all the usual. But I was too stunned to hear a whole lot of what he was saying. Then he totally switched gears

and started going on about how he was in love with her, maybe he should move to France with her . . . he even said I'd forced him into this sort of choice. "What are you getting so crazy about?" he yelled. "I'm a man. Men have affairs all the time. Don't be so f——ing provincial."

Needless to say, the *au pair* left the next morning. By then, though, we'd both calmed down a little, and we finally decided to see a marriage counselor. Did *we* decide? Actually, *I* decided. Anyway, during our sessions, it soon came out that Fred had been sleeping with the girl all summer— and she wasn't the first. He'd had an affair with a married woman who lived in our apartment building, a former babysitter, a secretary at his office. I mean, how much do you need? But even after all that, I kept telling myself I should give him another chance. For one thing, I couldn't face the explaining I'd have to do—to my family, his family, our friends. Also, he'd gotten me to the point where I felt like a total incompetent. He was unbelievably critical— somehow, he always made me feel that I wasn't as cool as he, or as classy or as well educated. I felt almost grateful that he'd put up with me for so long; what other man would want such a loser?

But when I found out he was at it again—this time with one of his freelancers—I knew that no matter what happened to me, even if I was alone for the rest of my life, I simply couldn't take it anymore. Here was a man who'd never been faithful, who was incapable of being faithful. . . . I just didn't want to live like that.

Separating from Fred was the hardest thing I've ever done—there were days I could barely get out of bed. I worried terribly about the children, too, and for good reason. Thanks to Fred, they'd seen me as this laughable ditz practically since they were born; so without him around during the week—he had them on weekends—they were pretty impossible. But I kept telling myself that *nothing could be worse* than the way it had been, and after a while, it got better. The kids settled down, I've recently started my own small public relations agency—a major step for me—and I'm even dating a little. There's one man in particular, who may not be as charismatic or handsome as Fred, but he's sweet and funny, and good with the kids. Will we ever marry? It's far too soon to tell. Besides, I'm not thinking about marriage right now; I'm concentrating mostly on myself.

I'm honestly so much happier now, I sometimes feel like a different person. And in fact, I *am* a different person, or learning to be. It's true what they say—there *is* life after divorce. I know. I'm living it.

Even when a relationship isn't as blatantly destructive as Marisa's was with her husband, "bad" reasons can keep it going long after it's served its purpose. Counselor Daphne Kingma notes that "the truth is that the creation of ourselves is what is really occurring under the charmed umbrella of our romantic relationships." She goes on to say that "relationships help us accomplish our *emotional* developmental tasks," and that they always end for a reason—they end when the developmental tasks have been completed by one or both of the partners."

Possibly, you have completed those tasks, and you really would be better off if you moved on. This isn't to say that you should suddenly accuse a loving but at the moment sexually scrambled husband of "stifling your potential," but it *is* something to consider. Do you really want to fight to get back a man who bores you to tears, or who, as the saying goes, didn't "grow" while you did? So, hard as it is, think it through. Whether your relationship has simply done its work or is so painful you can't bear another hour of anguish, maybe your man has actually done you a favor by forcing you to take a close look at its dynamics. Try hard not to let fear of such factors as loneliness, change, or the opinions of others stop you from taking that look—and acting on it if necessary.

"Our relationship wasn't bad, exactly; it was just sort of nonexistent," says Andrea, a thirty-seven-year-old textile designer:

We'd gotten married right after college, and while increasingly, my career absorbed me, Jake's floundered. He tried Wall Street, banking, advertising, but nothing really worked. It wasn't just a question of money; it was the drain of living with someone who had no focus, no joy in what he was doing. I'd come home all pumped up about a new design I'd done, dying to share it, and there would be Jake, slumped in front of the TV, looking miserable. I knew it would only make him feel worse if I talked to him about my work, so more and more, I didn't talk to him at all—about work or about the funny thing a co-worker had said or about anything. Jake had always been quiet, and when I'd met him, at only eighteen and in my first year of college, I equated "quiet" with deep. But as I got older, I began to have the uneasy feeling that maybe there wasn't quite as much to Jake as I'd thought. Still, I kept telling myself that a lot of women had it worse—he wasn't abusive, he didn't interfere much in my life. Besides, I couldn't imagine *not* being married. For years, Jake had always been there, like the off-white couch from Conran's, or the Tiffany lamp my parents had given us as a wedding present. I was used to him, all our friends were used to him. I don't know. It just seemed easier to stay together.

When out of nowhere, Jake told me he wanted to move in with a girl he'd met at the library, where he was researching different careers, at first I was shocked and, yes, hurt. But then, after he'd left and the days turned into weeks, I felt this enormous sense of relief, as if a huge weight had been lifted from me. Even the sky looked bluer.

One reason I'd stayed married was that I'd always covered for Jake with friends and our families. I'd told everyone how intelligent and sensitive he was, and how he just needed to find himself. Somehow, I couldn't face that cover being blown. But after we separated, I discovered that most of our friends had been very aware of Jake's problems, despite all my maneuvering. And my mother actually cried—with *relief*—when I told her he'd moved out. She'd been frantic all those years, watching me, as she put it, "lying to myself."

Once in a while, in the beginning, I'd come home from work and miss Jake's presence, but that was all. We were both better off without each other—and I knew it.

Does deciding you don't want this man back mean you'll be celibate for the rest of your life? Hardly. The male-female ratio has shifted dramatically according to the U.S. Census Bureau. While there were 93 men for every 100 women in 1970, by 1990, there were 108 men for every 100 women. Because the whole balance of dating and mating power has changed, no woman has to feel desperate. The men are definitely out there. All you have to do is get yourself in the right frame of mind and you'll have a good chance of connecting with whatever it is you want.

Assuming you've made the difficult decision to separate, find a good lawyer and get on with it. There is plenty of evidence that when a couple is divorcing, the man is most generous toward the wife early on in the proceedings, and the same goes for palimony suits. He's probably feeling guilty because of the other woman, and if he's any kind of a man at all, he's worried about how you—and the kids, if any—are going to manage. So act fast and get the settlement behind you so you can start living. This isn't grasping—it's just practical.

If, on the other hand, after a lot of soul searching, you truly feel the foundation of your relationship is solid, that you basically love and admire who he is (even though you're going through total hell at the moment), that you probably do want to spend the rest of your life with him, then it's imperative that you try to understand why he did what he did. If you avoid confronting the possibilities, however painful they may be, you'll never be able to forgive the man or move on to a richer, more rewarding relationship. Because when he does come back, your relationship with him will not be the same. Better, you hope, but not the same.

CHAPTER 3

Why Did

He Do It?

The Big Ten

Okay, you've taken a hard, objective, look at this man and he's passed the Desert Island Test, at least for now. (Also, you can't think of many other men who would, except maybe Kevin Costner, and he's taken.) Your instincts tell you that despite recent events, the qualities you once found so endearing are still lurking there somewhere, so the relationship is probably worth saving.

Your next job, then, is to try to figure out why he strayed in the first place; the more insights you have, the better equipped you'll be to deal. Remember, even if the two of you have already talked it over, and he's tried to explain, he may not understand his real motivations himself, so he's hardly going to be able to make them clear to you. No matter. Do a little sleuthing on your own by studying this vital rundown.

The ten major reasons a man winds up in another woman's bed are:

THE MID-LIFE "IS THAT ALL THERE IS?" SYNDROME

The term *mid-life crisis* has practically become a cliché, like PMS or "significant other." But knowing how common the problem is doesn't help much when you've got a man on your hands who's going through one. The term refers to that treacherous period, usually between the ages of forty and fifty, when a man wakes up one morning and thinks, "There's got to be more to life than this." He then starts behaving like a tortured sixteen-year-old, raging hormones and all. Maybe his hair has begun thinning out, or his high school basketball shorts are three inches too small in the waist, or the new receptionist just yawned when he gallantly welcomed her to the firm. Whatever the catalyst, he's a man who suddenly feels his looks, charm, and sex appeal are slipping, that adventure and passion are passing him by. What he's desperate to do is test his powers, make certain "that he is still potent, still capable of 'conquering' the heroines of his youthful days," says British sociologist Annette Lawson in her book, *Adultery: An Analysis of Love and Betrayal.*

This is also the time he starts questioning life, as he faces (or rather, tries not to face) his own mortality. Remember that marvelous scene in the film *Moonstruck,* when the husband, played by Vincent Gardenia, comes home after an evening with his mistress, and his wife, acted by the incomparable Olympia Dukakis, looks him in the eye and says, "I just want you to know, no matter what you do, you're going to die just like everyone else." The wife knew very well what she was up against . . . and by showing him she knew, and understood what he was feeling (not liked or accepted it; just understood it), proved herself a pretty tough lady to leave.

What you're really dealing with here is a man who's having a lot of trouble with the idea of aging—one of the reasons that he almost always seeks out a much younger woman as a lover.

"The typical story is this," noted California psychologist Zev Wanderer in "Why Husbands Don't Leave Their Wives," an article in the April, 1989 issue of *Cosmopolitan*. "He's been married a number of years, he's leading a humdrum life, and suddenly he meets someone at work. She's single, invariably younger, and there's an instant attraction. He's been on a treadmill, and this is the most exciting thing that's ever happened to him."

"Men particularly have a problem when they reach middle age," said well-known California divorce attorney, Marvin Mitchelson, in the same article. "If they've been working hard, they feel as if they've missed out on the good things in life. They really want their pleasure—want to indulge it before it is too late. They look at someone younger, and they want a second chance."

Why younger? Because in everything from magazines to movies, the idea that young equals sexy and desirable is constantly hammered home. It's therefore no wonder that even very stable people—men *and* women—feel less attractive as they age. But for a man, virility is far more tied in with total identity. It spells power, at least in his head, and when he sees a gray hair or notices he's developing a small pot, he goes crazy. Seemingly overnight (although he's probably been building up to it for years), he turns into a sexual vampire—hell-bent on sucking the last drop of youth out of any twentysomething fox who's available.

Since in this case "available" means single—married women in their twenties are usually too wrapped up in the fun of being newly married to fool around—you have double trouble on your hands: she is not only younger, she's unattached. But before you start investigating facelifts and collagen shots, let's deal with your head first. Consider that somewhere, deep down, your man has to know that she's not going to make *him* any younger. In fact, as time passes, all those girlish references to Guns and Roses and Vanilla Ice will make him feel *older*. What's more, the odds are that he's well aware he has a lot to lose, both emotionally and financially, by playing house with a mere child.

SAME OLD SAFE SEX

The term *safe sex* has meaning more far-reaching than simply use of a condom. If, for quite a while, you've "submitted" to lovemaking on Saturday nights at ten-fifteen, your mind on such pressing domestic matters as little Alex's lost Ninja Turtle, while she's only too eager to tear off her slinky teddy and try any-thing . . . what woman wouldn't be in trouble? Nobody's blaming you, and of course *she* doesn't have to worry about Ninja Turtles (or mortgage payments, or the ominous leak in the dining room ceiling), so comparing yourself with her won't do anybody any good. But sex often does become a pretty low priority during marriage or a long-term relationship. There are so many other things to think about—money, work, the kids, the house—that it can get lost in the day-to-day life crush. Bed becomes a place to sleep, not a place to frolic or connect.

Were you a little cool in bed before all this happened? Perhaps on some subconscious level you sensed his imminent withdrawal and have been trying to protect yourself by pretending you didn't care. Or maybe you're withholding sex as a way to deal with anger. Whatever's going on, try to take an honest look at it. If you indeed have the sneaky suspicion that the main reason your man went elsewhere for sex is that you had a highly questionable number of headaches (as in "not tonight, dear"), you might want to set aside pride and just tackle him. An evening of hot, urgent sex has turned a lot of relationships around.

"I know Linda is exhausted after working all day and putting the kids to bed," a lawyer we talked with said rather wistfully, "but sex was one of the best things we had going, and I hate that it's become such a once-in-a-while thing. The simple fact is, I need more sex, and if I can't get it at home, I'm going to get it somewhere. I just wish she knew I'd rather be getting it with her."

Some men turn to other women for sex because they're just plain curious. Youth isn't the only big focus in our culture; we live in a world where sex sells. Think of some of the steamy doings you've seen recently in movies and on TV; print ads and magazine and newspaper articles only add to the heat. It's easy to see why a man who didn't fool around much before marriage might be intrigued—he wants a piece of what the rest of the world is doing. If he's too shy or inhibited to play out his fantasies with you—or if you don't seem all that interested—he may turn to a stranger for fun. If this is your case, try to get him to tell you what he really wants in bed, and then go for it, assuming that what he wants isn't either painful or threatening to you. Sometimes, even if it is a little weird, you can work out a variation on the theme. When Isabelle, a forty-five-year-old interior decorator from Beverly Hills, discovered that making love to two women at once was her errant husband's ultimate fantasy, she pretended to *be* two women—one a tigress, the other all trembly and passive. They never actually acted on the fantasy for real, but just talking about it, plus Isabelle's willingness to go along (on her own terms), opened up all sorts of sexy new possibilities— and the other woman was soon history.

It's also worth noting that not only is sex big on the big screen but adultery is particularly hot—a whopping 60 percent of movies deal with the topic. Generally, this "juiciest of all forbidden fruits," as it was recently described on a Fox TV show called, appropriately enough, *When Your Spouse Is a Louse,* comes off looking pretty terrific. Affairs are supposed to be good for people. At the very least, they're a lot more fun than driving straight home and taking out the lawn mower. Add to this the fact that everybody from celebs to moguls to the British royal family seems to be happily "doing it," and it takes a very strong man not to be influenced. As The Donald goes, so goes the nation.

Since sex is such a delicate issue—even more so when a couple is in crisis—we've devoted a whole chapter to it later. For now, it's enough to start thinking about what may currently be lacking in the erotic arena, and what you can do to get the good times rolling again.

BECAUSE IT WAS THERE

What? You mean he actually went to bed with that bimbo in accounting just because they wound up at the convention together? It happens a lot more often than most women think. To a surprising number of men, a quickie is no big deal, and has nothing to do with their feelings for their wives. This isn't the most pleasant fact to face, but it's the truth. If you've just found out that your man has had a couple of one-night stands, maybe even with the same woman, it's best to be low-keyed about it. Actually, if you're almost certain he's only fooled around once or twice, sometimes it's better not to mention it at all. If you can't handle that, however—sophistication be damned; you'd like to tear the bitch's eyes out and hobble her—then go ahead and discuss it. If he instantly confesses, assures you that the incident meant nothing to him, and swears he'll never do it again, then *believe him.* There's little sadder than the outraged wife who dashes off to a divorce lawyer and blows a whole marriage or relationship over a relatively minor indiscretion or two.

Even though it may take some temporary readjusting, forgiveness really is the way to go. After all, you two have an investment in each other. He loves you, needs you, makes you laugh, knows where not to tickle you . . . and he may not even remember her last name.

THE TREADMILL FACTOR

A man may begin to feel his life has become a droning round of the same work, same friends, same food, same couch-potato nights in front of the TV. So he starts craving change, adventure— anything but another night of *L.A. Law.* Unlike men caught up in a classic mid-life crisis, these boys aren't so much wrestling with fears of getting older as with boredom. For them, it equals bondage, and bondage makes the male heart wander (except for the kinky few).

To such men, another woman—almost any other woman—seems exciting. And sometimes she is. There's a type, rampant in big cities, who always know about that fabulous little jazz club tucked away on a seductive mean street, or who used to be a dancer and once dated Baryshnikov. Never mind that she's addicted to shopping, and if her parents weren't still supporting her, she'd be carrying all her belongings in a Gucci shopping bag and sleeping in doorways—she spells glamour. Mystery. And any man who sees himself as locked into routines—routines that are a constant reminder his life hasn't added up to what he'd hoped for—is particularly vulnerable.

So there he is, feeling caught in the labyrinth of everyday life, and suddenly there *she* is—ready to charm him, flatter him, fuss over him, make him feel like the virile, desirable young hunk he once was, or saw himself as. These are ego boosters he may not have gotten from you in quite a while.

Then, too, even when a marriage or relationship is basically good, it requires a lot of compromise, patience, selflessness—all sterling qualities, but a man can get tired of making the effort on a full-time basis. What he wants is to stop playing saint and start having some fun.

"I never intended to get emotionally involved, and neither did she," says Larry, a fifty-two-year-old investment banker, of his affair with a thirty-seven-year-old freelance artist. "We just had a great time together. Neither of us expected anything. Chloe didn't care about getting into the country club. I wasn't after home-cooked meals. We had no goals, except to make each other feel good. Sure, it was 'immature,' but that's precisely why it worked. Nobody had to take out the garbage."

"Denise made me feel so alive," adds John, a thirty-six-year-old civil engineer. "I could be my real self with her—you know, kind of wild and funny and sensitive, all at the same time—which was a far cry from the plodding provider I'd become in my wife's eyes. And I could tell Denise things I could never tell my wife—let her in on fears, dreams. . . . I guess it was because she didn't have any script for our relationship. She really didn't want anything from me, except for us to enjoy each other and be relaxed. That made all the difference. I didn't have to pretend about anything."

Such men aren't so much looking outside of their primary relationships for what they feel is missing, as they are simply looking for an outlet. The problem is, though, they soon discover that as a steady diet, the "outlet" can be pretty hard to take. Everybody needs quiet time—even astronauts have to stop doing somersaults and take a Tang break, right? Fun isn't fun when it's relentless; it's just another treadmill.

Consciously or not, your man probably already senses that. Yes, his life with you may be a touch predictable, but it's also comfortable. And although his new girlfriend may look carefree by candlelight, unless he's a total idiot he has to know she wouldn't be a Julia Roberts clone after spending a day as cub scout den mother, either. He knows, even if he's trying to deny it right now, that somebody has to take out the garbage.

THE PRESSURE COOKER CRUNCH

Now, for the flip side of the Treadmill Factor. Maybe all those grown-up responsibilities like mortgage payments, competition at work, your children's tuition, car payments, or constant deadlines have become too much for him. It's not the routines in his life but the pressures that are getting to him. He may therefore have concluded that the sexy little trainee in marketing is just what he needs to keep him from exploding.

In an article called "Broken Ties" that appeared in the November, 1990, issue of *New Woman*, Frank Pittman pointed out that sometimes, "Married men fall in love when reality begins to overwhelm them: for example, when their first child is born, when they lose their job, when they get rich, their parents die, or their health starts to fail. You might fall in love just to avoid dealing with some of the problems in your life. Falling in love is like a period of temporary insanity. At times, it looks as if falling in love is what people do when they don't think they can keep living their lives, but are not quite ready to commit suicide! In time the obsesssion will pass. . . ."

But obsession is what you're up against. Men caught up in a high-pressure life-style, or who just feel they're under tremendous strain, often try to create a brand new reality for themselves by having an affair.

"For some people, it is adultery, not marriage, that is reality," explains sociologist Annette Lawson.

The new reality is based more on the person he'd like to be than on the person he is. Lawson goes on to say that "far from *always* being something chaotic, experienced as a loss of control over one's own life, adultery is often a way in which the world is actually *reordered* according to strongly held beliefs about the proper relationship between women and men. The marriage comes to be seen as where the chaos is; the alternative relationship one where sense and meaning are rediscovered or perhaps discovered for the first time." Lawson concludes that "the adulterous spouse may experience the liaison itself as reassuring about the stability and rightness of the world during a particularly stressful period."

If this is your present situation, try to keep in mind the tremendous pressure your man is experiencing, and that he clearly doesn't know how to handle it. Here's how Gary, a forty-five-year-old builder, describes his feelings:

> I really don't know what came over me. Maureen and I had a pretty good marriage, at least compared to most of the people in our neighborhood. She's always been supportive of me, even when I couldn't give her some of the things her girlfriends had. She's kept herself in shape; she's never once said no to sex. So you could say that what I did had nothing to do with her. It was right after our oldest son started college. The financial pressures were really getting to me, even though he was on partial scholarship. I was behind with car payments, too, and then the boss announced he was going to have to lay off ten people. I wasn't one of them, thank God, but he said he might have

to lay off more if business didn't pick up. Well, I was about ready to lose it. I couldn't face going home, so I asked this waitress I knew from the coffee shop to meet me for a drink when she got off work. She did, and, as they say, nature took its course, and now I feel terrible. I never wanted it to get serious, but it kind of has—the sleeping together part, anyway. This is a small town, and I'm scared that Maureen is going to find out, and then what'll I do? As if things weren't bad enough before!

Gary has more insight into the reasons for his philandering than many men do (although at the moment, that isn't stopping him). But whether or not your husband or lover understands why he's doing what he's doing, what he needs is support. Encourage him to talk to you about the pressures he's under, and be your warmest, most loving self as you help him figure out how to handle them. You can bet that with everything else he has on his mind, he'd rather have you as his escape value. It would certainly be easier than going to the trouble of scheduling secret rendezvous.

Try not to add to his pressures, as well. Forget the new refrigerator and worries about Jimmy's over'.ite for now, and concentrate on making your home an oasis of soothing calm. Even more important, *be* one.

DON'T CROWD ME

Some men (women too, for that matter), are uncomfortable with true intimacy. The drama, suspense, or thrill of a double life is therefore extremely seductive; it keeps them from having to get too close to either you *or* the other woman. If you were at a stage in your relationship where you were demanding more intimacy than you'd been getting, your man may have panicked. Having an affair is his way of avoiding the issue altogether. This type of man usually comes from a home in which male-female roles were rigidly defined—his parents weren't so much a loving, tender, trusting couple as they were Father–Primary Wage Earner and Mother–Housewife. Often, he truly longs to have a closer relationship with you but doesn't know how to bring it about; since his own parents dealt on such a superficial level, he hasn't even seen how a healthy, loving alliance works. Again, it's vital to understand what he's feeling, because that's the only way you're going to be able to help him get to the point where he's not afraid to open up.

One thing you can count on: if his new relationship starts getting "too close" he'll be out the door—and very probably into the arms of *another* other woman. L.A. author Marion Zola puts it this way: "The same reasons that drove this type of husband to one outside woman now push him to yet another. An affair is a good means of avoiding intimacy in marriage. Similarly, a new lover protects a man from getting too near his old one. Taking off before the woman does allows such a man to feel in complete control."

You've got to feel sorry for these men, because they obviously don't like themselves very much to begin with. They need a woman's love and approval, but feel they don't deserve it. The idea of closeness in a relationship, with its attendant qualities of openness and trust, makes them uncomfortable; it conjures up painful ambivalence about wanting love, yet feeling unlovable.

In an interview with a thirty-nine-year-old editor at a men's magazine, fear of closeness comes across with poignant clarity. John began by talking about his eight-month relationship with a teacher at his daughter's school:

> Suddenly, all my wife ever seemed to want to discuss was our relationship, how we never really shared anything, never really communicated, and I was getting tired of it. So when I met this teacher at a parent conference, and she seemed receptive, I jumped at the chance. And at first it was great. We got together on weekends here and there, during the week for drinks, and once in a while, she'd take a few days off and go on business trips with me. She was

really cute and funny, and we made each other laugh. The problem was, though, she was thirty-four, the clock was ticking, if you know what I mean, and she wanted a real relationship, a family of her own. I couldn't blame her, but the last thing I wanted was more talk about "relationships," and the idea of playpens and midnight feedings all over again made me want to take off for Mozambique. So I told her we'd have to end it. She took it kind of hard, which surprised me, because I thought she was just in it for the fun, too.

I wouldn't mind having another affair; in fact, I'm sure I will. It relieves the pressure at home, and sex is always better when it's new. I don't ever plan to leave my wife, but I'm sort of a randy guy, and I really don't see any harm as long as no one gets hurt.

If his wife finds out about his affairs, of course, she's certainly going to be hurt, and it doesn't sound as if his girlfriend took the break-up so lightly, either. But men like this usually aren't able even to imagine how the other person feels. They're too busy trying to stay loose, be cool, and hide out from deeper feelings.

If your man falls into this category, remember that he'll almost certainly not leave you for real—you're a vital part of his avoidance package. Try not to crowd him (easy to say when you're ready to kill him, but try anyway), but at the same time, let him know you'll no longer put up with such behavior. Be loving but firm—if you have kids, you already know it's possible to be both. It helps to remember how frightened and insecure he is underneath all the swagger. Once he feels safer with you—and this may take some doing—chances are he'll begin to see he can risk opening up a little . . . and that maybe he's more lovable than he knows. Then he won't have to keep running from you, and from a series of other women, to avoid intimacy—he'll start embracing it.

DEPRESSION

Everybody gets a little depressed now and then, but sometimes a man suddenly and inexplicably loses his zest for life; the very idea of getting through another day seems almost more than he can bear. Psychologists say depression is caused by repressing anger, which puts us in a state of mind where we feel helpless, impotent, unable to make things happen. The easy way out, then, is to *make* something happen—and for some men that means finding a woman who'll be sympathetic, sexy . . . and offer an escape from realities that are causing the depression in the first place. What they don't foresee is that the fix won't work.

One man told us he'd been so utterly miserable he wasn't even sure whether or not he wanted to go on living. Then, at a basketball game with some of his pals, he saw "a girl dressed all in red, not a beautiful girl, but she had a great body and a wonderful smile," and he felt he just "had" to have her. "It was like an obsession," he remembers. "I really made a fool of myself that night, because she came with a date, but I just couldn't help it. She wouldn't give me her phone number—I followed her when she went to get a hot dog, and just point blank asked her for it—but I did find out her name, and I called every Sally Hancock in the phone book until I found her. At first, she thought I was some kind of a nut, but I finally convinced her to meet me for lunch, and that was the beginning."

When the affair ended after only a month, Matthew sank even deeper into depression. He cried a lot, would eat only an occasional sandwich, finally refused even to leave the house. Luckily, his frantic wife was able to talk him into getting therapy, where he's spent the last year-and-a-half analyzing the true causes of his depression—feelings of sexual inadequacy and rage at an overbearing father, just to name two.

If you suspect that your husband or lover is trying to cope with chronic depression by having a fling, be calm, be confident, and above all, be careful. He's fragile right now, and you've got to be supportive, plus gently encourage him to seek professional help. Perhaps long-term therapy won't be necessary—it often isn't—but depression is serious and should be treated as such. Even though he may think he's going to find the solution to all his troubles in the arms of another woman, you know that's not the case. (On some level, he probably does, too.) And letting him *know* that you know, and that you care about him, want to help him, should propel him toward the therapy he needs.

REVENGE

Remember when you were at the barbecue last summer, and your neighbor started really coming on to you? You tried to extricate yourself, but your husband accused you of flirting—couldn't stop talking about it for weeks. Or what about the time you got an innocent call from a long-ago boyfriend and he pulled the receiver out of your hand and threw the phone across the room? Or maybe at one point during your relationship you actually *were* involved with another man, and months, or even years later, he still hasn't forgiven or forgotten. In such cases, he may try to pay you back by flaunting his own affair.

"It's always amazed me how much more forgiving women are than men when it comes to infidelity—or what seems like infidelity," says Carl, a twenty-six-year-old computer analyst. "I've been caught by girlfriends more than once, and they've usually tried hard to understand why I did it. But let me even suspect my woman has been with someone else, and that's it. Either I don't want to have anything more to do with her, or I decide to get even. The funny thing is, though, that when I do sleep with someone else out of revenge, there's no pleasure in it. I just want *her* to find out so she'll feel bad."

Indeed, affairs motivated by revenge rarely turn out to be much fun for anyone involved. Jordan, a thirty-five-year-old sportswriter, told us that when he found out his wife had had an affair with a man from her office a few years before, he virtually went berserk: "I couldn't believe she'd do that to me, so the very same week, I picked up a girl in a bar and took her to a motel—never even called home. When I finally came in at about four A.M., my wife was wide awake, and asked where I'd been. I just said 'out.' That really got to her."

Such actions seem pretty rotten—in fact, they are—but surprisingly, this sort of philandering doesn't have to be a major threat to a relationship. If he's simply trying to get even for some imagined or acutal indiscretion of yours, he's obviously still in love with you. Why else would he want you to know how much you've hurt him? The problem is, *you're* not so sure that's it, especially in cases where you had no idea you were making him jealous. All you know is that he's fooling around with a twenty-year-old Madonna wanna-be. But think: How did he react when you were—admit it—flirting with that cute gas station attendant? True, all you did was make a suggestive little quip about the hot rod he was working on, but did your man glower? Clench his teeth? Zoom out onto the highway at ninety miles an hour? There *were* clues; you just weren't paying attention.

Once you've pinpointed the fact that he's making something out of nothing, start talking. Tell him you love only him, that you've been a hopeless flirt since stroller days, but now that you know how much it bothers him, you'll stop. This should also put an end to his desire for revenge.

On the other hand, if there has been someone else in your life during this relationship, then you'll have to figure out what you weren't getting from it, and what you two can do to make it better. Remember that you've hurt *him* just as much as he's hurt *you,* so don't come on like the Betrayed Woman, all huffy and high-minded.

LACK OF ATTENTION

When was the last time you really noticed your husband or lover—not as the shadow who pays part or all of your living expenses, not as a free escort service, but as a *man?* What about all those things you used to love to do together—white-water rafting on the Delaware, staying up half the night to play gin for ten cents a point, meeting after work for a leisurely stroll through the park? Whatever happened to the delight you used to take in his company, the lavish compliments on his sense of humor, charm, abandon in bed? Of course you still care (the proof is that you're not at all pleased by this latest development), but be honest: Does he still know it?

"She looks at me and doesn't see me," says a fifty-one-year-old movie producer.

> And it's sad, because it used to be so good. When we were first married, the sex was fantastic; even up until a couple of years ago, it was one of the best parts of our relationship. We used to do so many things together, too. Sometimes we'd have a picnic in the woods near our house, or we'd go skinny-dipping in the pond.... Once we drove a hundred miles on a whim to get some Mexican food at a little place we'd been to on vacation. But now she's always too tired. It's not that I don't appreciate how hard she works—she's the vice-president of a big design consulting firm—it's just that for all the attention I get, I might as well not be around. But with Sarah, it's like starting over— she really listens when I talk, laughs at my jokes, seems to *want* to sleep with me. It's not like she's doing me a favor, the way it is with my wife.

Maybe you're so used to having your man there, like the old oak tree in the backyard, you've forgotten he's a vulnerable human being with needs that cry out for fulfillment just as much as your own. Is it possible that he's sought another woman because he craves the affection and approval he hasn't been getting at home? Then for goodness sake, start giving them to him! With a little attention on your part, the odds are that he'll be relieved to come back. Flattery, affection—they'll only get a woman everywhere. Is there any reason he should have to look outside his primary relationship for such signs of love?

YOUR BASIC WANDERER

It's possible that your man has always had a roving eye—he's just a man who loves the ladies (at least, that's what he tells himself). Often, the signs of wanderlust were always there, but you may have overlooked them, either because it was a whirlwind courtship and you didn't have time to look, or because you didn't want to believe he was the type to whom variety was necessary, the spice of life. Unlike men who use affairs as a way to avoid intimacy, these men see themselves as a combination of Mickey Rourke, Matt Dillon, and Sean Penn, with a dash of Marlon Brando in *The Wild One* tossed in.

"Continuous, compulsive secret infidelity (philandering) is a well-known macho pattern," notes Frank Pittman, "but it actually occurs in only a small percent of intact marriages. Philanderers are mostly men who fear female control and are in love with their masculinity. They believe there is a gender war going on and they want to be on the winning team, so they score with each woman in turn, tag her, and discard her. They aren't good at marriage since it requires honesty and equality with a female partner. It would be inappropriate to consider any of this 'normal.' "

Marjorie, a thirty-one-year-old hairstylist, still shudders when she remembers life with her first husband.

> We were both only twenty when we got married. And when we had our first child a year later, I think Steve felt way too tied down too soon. He was one of those super-macho guys, hot-tempered and kind of wild, but at first, I told myself the wildness was part of his charm. I was proud when other women stared at him as we walked down the street. It was, like, *they* wanted him, but *I* had him. I thought maybe he was fooling around a little at work, but that didn't bother me too much, either—I figured that was just what men did.
>
> But then girls started calling him at home, and one day

a friend of mine told me she'd seen Steve all over town with a woman we'd both met at the Jersey shore on vacation. So I started snooping and found motel receipts hidden in the back of his closet, pictures of the two of them, even a love letter. That night I really let him have it, told him it had to be her or me. At one point I even started punching him, I was so mad, but he just laughed and held me off. After a while, though, he blew up—said who did I think I was, telling him what to do? Another word and he'd be out the door, and then where did I think I'd be? I had an eighteen-month-old toddler, and another baby on the way . . . besides, I still loved the man.

So we settled down, but then I found out Steve was seeing someone else, and a couple of months later it was someone else; once he even moved in with a girl, a flight attendant, for a couple of weeks. This went on for four years, and all along, the crazy thing was, he didn't see anything wrong with it. If my father hadn't found out what was going on, and packed me and the kids up and taken us over to his house, swearing he was going to go after Steve with a shotgun, I'd probably still be with him.

Now that I have what I call a real marriage, to a man who's honest and caring, I can't believe I put up with what I did for so long. When a guy is chronically unfaithful, it eats away at your self-esteem, and pretty soon, whether you realize it or not, you're a basket case.

It's worth mentioning that some women—a very few—seem able to handle this looser-than-usual life-style. (Most, however, tend to be involved with rich men, and have reached some sort of mutually open agreement—meaning they get to fool around, too). But no matter how together they seem on the outside, you have to wonder about the state of their self-esteem. If you're one of the rare women who can play this sort of game, okay; but if not, you're going to have to face the fact that your man has a real problem. He's so afraid of being controlled by a woman, he'll look at you suspiciously if you ask whether he wants Swiss or

Cheddar on his hamburger. He's not about to start "sharing" where he was last night. He needs therapy if he's to change, but the problem is, urging him to seek it is usually seen as yet another attempt to pull the strings. You can try it, of course, or, probably better, get into therapy yourself and find out how to deal with your own feelings as well as with him. Sometimes, threatening to leave him if he doesn't shape up—and meaning it—will shock him into reform.

CHAPTER 4

To Confront

or Not

Now that you have a pretty good idea of why he's doing what he's doing, the big question is: Do you confront him or not?

For some women, of course, this issue is moot: your man may have already told you he's involved with someone else, and perhaps he has even moved in with her. Or maybe the signs that he was having an affair were so obvious and hurtful, you confronted him soon after you noticed them—not as a tactic in your quest to get him back, but because you were so outraged and furious, you just couldn't help yourself.

If you have already confronted your husband or lover, and possibly in a way you wish you hadn't, try not to worry too much. Your emotions at that moment were overpowering, so even if you screamed and cried and fired half his belongings across the bedroom, it's okay. You were operating out of honest anger and passion—two perfectly normal responses under the circumstances, and ones that can be quite seductive, because they show you care. Besides, people are only human, and you're "people," aren't you?

If, on the other hand, he told you about the affair, and you were so stunned and taken aback you barely reacted at all, don't tear yourself apart, either. You still have lots of time to respond.

But what if he hasn't yet told you about his affair, and you haven't yet told him you're sure about what he's up to? What to do then? It's only natural to be afraid of bringing up so painful and potentially explosive a subject. You don't know if he'll storm out the door for good, tell you things you don't want to hear, such as why he looked for someone else in the first place, or lie blatantly. Sometimes it seems better simply to do nothing, and let the affair run its course. That way, you reason, you avoid the risks inherent in confrontation, and by not pushing him to the wall, have a better chance of getting him back in the end.

When it comes to confrontation, even expert opinion varies. Some professionals feel confrontation will only lead to your becoming a casualty in this most painful of love wars—sociologist Annette Lawson, who's done extensive research on extramarital affairs, goes so far as to suggest that it can be "profoundly damaging," causing reactions from "violence to divorce"—but the majority think confrontation is a virtual must.

"Affairs thrive on secrecy," comments Frank Pittman. "The conspiracy and adventure and tricks produce an alliance in the affair, while the lies and deceit increase the discomfort at home. All of us feel bound to those who share our secrets and uncomfortable with those to whom we are lying." The very *power* of an affair, Pittman notes, may be in its secrecy. That is especially true if the weakness of the marriage or relationship is in its avoidance of issues, including the issue that's paramount in your mind at the moment—the fact that your man is having an affair with another woman.

Only you, of course, can assess both the situation and your man, but at the very least, confrontation allows you to operate from a position of strength. (Besides, what do you do with all that rage if you simply suffer in silence? You turn it inward, and only add to your anguish.) By bringing the affair out into the open, you can fight it, both fairly and, yes, a little unfairly when indicated. Letting him know that you know creates an opportunity for honest talk, the chance to develop a new level of intimacy—if not at this very minute, then in the future. One woman we spoke with even went so far as to say that the night she confronted her husband was the first time they had *ever* really talked, and he felt that way, too.

"A direct confrontation can have an unexpected effect," notes Diane Vaughan, sociologist and author, in *Uncoupling: How Relationships Come Apart.* "The two interact, perhaps with an intensity that has long been absent. This sudden intense exchange can remind the initiator (of the breakup) of the other person's good traits and the ties that exist between them. In addition, the partner, perhaps for the first time, has the opportunity to present details about the couple's life together that the initiator has underplayed, forgotten, or ignored.... The partner poses alternative explanations that contradict the negative history of the partner and relationship that the initiator has been constructing."

Confrontation, then, provides one of the very best chances you'll get to remind your husband or lover of what is good about both you and the relationship, and to convince him that the relationship really can work. He will no longer be able to see you as controlling, self-involved, inattentive (or whatever other negatives he's talking himself into believing you have) because there you are, facing him, showing none of those qualities. Rather, you are showing love—even if you're fighting mad—and the willingness to try again, to make the relationship better. He will no longer be able to tell himself that you "never went anywhere together" as a couple, or that "the kids always came first," or that "he had to practically beg you to have sex" because you will force him to remember the unforgettable two weeks in Tuscany, the time you parked the children with his mother so you could go along on one of his sales trips to Akron, the night you surprised him with a copy of the *Kama Sutra* and tried out just about every position in it. Bringing him back to reality in this way is a vital step in your attempt to save the relationship.

Pretending an affair isn't happening, adds Pittman, also "puts people in the position of not having to acknowledge problems or do anything to solve them." While it's completely understandable that in the beginning, many women will do anything to avoid such a painful truth—cannot even contemplate the emotional turmoil they know they must go through if they do face it—the results of maintaining this posture are usually even more devastating. You are left feeling overwhelmingly helpless. By refusing to acknowledge the affair, and doing nothing about it, women are relinquishing control of their lives. In effect, they are saying they *have* no control—that outside events determine who they are and what will happen to them. Any woman who does that winds up playing Ultimate Victim, a role which, aside from being no help whatsoever in trying to get a man back, can only lead to grief.

"To be victimized," says California psychiatrist Wayne W. Dyer, in *Pulling Your Own Strings,* "means to be governed and checked by forces outside yourself; and while these forces are unquestionably ubiquitous in our culture, *you can rarely be victimized unless you allow it to happen.*"

Victims work hard at their game. A wife or girlfriend who is determined to ignore her man's affair must first convince herself that there *is* no problem, although all the signs are there: the late, late nights; the whispered phone conversations; the hang-up calls; the unexplained credit card charges; the shying away from sex. If awareness of the affair should surface, she immediately represses it, telling herself that it will all somehow simply go away, without any effort on her part. All this convincing and ignoring, however, takes its toll: so much energy is channeled into avoidance tactics, there's little left for anything else—work, friendships, outside interests, the very life elements so vital in helping her weather the crisis. Then, too, however hard she tries to deny knowledge of the affair, somewhere inside, she does know, and this "split" between truth and denial creates an even further energy drain. The point is, "ignorance" simply doesn't work. Pittman calls the idea that there is safety in ignorance of a spouse's affair "a myth." Perhaps some royals and politician's wives are able to successfully avert their eyes (although who knows what they're really going through?) but not most women. The emotional toll is too great, the loss of self-esteem too staggering.

Consider the effects of such denial on Jennifer, a thirty-nine-year-old elementary school teacher and mother of two young sons. "All my life, it seemed that other people had told me what to do," she remembers. "My mother was one of those Technicolor Ladies—opinionated, overpowering, larger than life. She made me feel, not stupid, exactly, but sort of dreary and not very interesting. I learned early on never to assert myself; the putdowns and sometimes even outright ridicule that invariably followed were too painful. My Dad wasn't much help; he was more like me—quiet and shy. Besides, it was just easier to do what she said."

When Jennifer married Tom, an outgoing, self-assured real estate broker, this childhood pattern almost immediately began repeating itself. It was Tom who decided where they would live, how they would budget their money, which friends they would entertain. Used to abdicating control to someone "stronger," Jennifer always gave in. And if occasionally she wondered why she so often felt unhappy and anxious, just as she had as a child, she quickly set such thoughts aside. After all, Tom was her husband; who better to run their lives?

It was hardly any wonder that when Tom began seeing a woman who worked at his office, Jennifer could not allow herself to admit it was happening. Having spent her entire life being dominated by others, she felt she had no right to react—and even if she had wanted to, she wouldn't have known how. "Besides," she says, "the idea of risking Tom's anger if I confronted him, or worse, risking the possibility that he might leave me, was too much for me to face." So she buried her pain, ignored the affair, and tried to go on about her life. Privately, she defended her actions: wasn't it worth a little abnegation to save her marriage?

But even though she seemed in control—the house immaculate, her sons never a second late for Little League, her manner solicitous whenever Tom was home—inside, Jennifer was frozen. Afraid to act, having no sense of herself as someone who could have any effect on what was happening to her, she simply shut down.

"Victims almost always operate from weakness," says Dyer. "They let themselves be dominated, pushed around, because they often feel they are not smart enough or strong enough to be in charge of their lives. So they hand their own strings over to someone "smarter" or "stronger," rather than take the risks involved in being self-assertive.

"You are a victim when your life is not working for you," Dyer goes on to say. "If you are behaving in self-defeating ways, if you are miserable, out of sorts, hurt, anxious, afraid to be yourself, or in other similar states which immobilize you, if you aren't functioning in a self-enhancing manner, or if you feel as if you are being manipulated by forces outside of yourself, then you are a victim—and it is my contention that your own victimization is never worth defending. If you agree, then you will be asking: What about relief from victimization? What about freedom?"

In Jennifer's case, "relief" came only after the horrifying moment she found herself in the bathroom, staring at a packet of razor blades—"mesmerized," she says.

> It was a hot August day; I remember that the air was so heavy and still, I could hear myself breathing. I was alone in the house—the boys were with friends, and Tom was out showing some properties, or so he said. I took a razor blade out of its wrapping and slid it tentatively along my wrist. It felt so cold, so final. The cut was tiny; it barely broke the skin. But something about seeing that thin line of blood woke me up, and I thought: "Am I actually going to *die* because I'm such a wimp I can't even stand up for myself? Why don't I just give this woman my husband, my children, my home and be done with it? The idea made me so mad that I threw the packet of blades into the wastebasket, showered, dressed, put a Band-Aid on my wrist

and drove over to Tom's office. Wonder of wonders, he was there, talking to two clients. As soon as they'd left, I went into his office and shut the door behind me. I felt—it's hard to explain—exhilarated, high, almost. After I'd gotten it all out—about the woman, and how I wasn't going to put up with it—he didn't say anything for a long time. He just kept looking at me strangely, as if he were seeing me for the first time. "What happened to your wrist?" he said finally. I was about to tell him I'd almost tried to commit suicide, but then something inside me screamed "No!" "A piece of broken glass in the dishwasher," I said. The last thing I wanted was his pity, and that made me proud of myself for the first time in a very long time.

After that, it isn't as if everything changed overnight, but he did give up the woman. And I stopped tiptoeing around and letting him make all the decisions. Actually, once he got used to it, he seemed rather relieved. He said that having to assume total responsibility had made him feel pretty burdened.

By taking on the role of victim and refusing to acknowledge your man's affair, you also help perpetuate the backstreet thrills. As in childhood, being "bad" loses a lot of its kicks once the fear of getting caught is removed. Would Tom Sawyer have had so much fun if he hadn't had to *sneak* off to see Huckleberry Finn? What if Aunt Polly had simply said: "Have a good time, dear!" handed him a picnic basket, and shown him the front door? You're not hoping your man will have a good time, of course—you're praying for the exact opposite—but the principle is the same. Confrontation minimizes, and often all but eliminates, the sense of adventure most men find so exciting about having an affair because it removes the secrecy element.

After being confronted, your man won't have to look furtively up and down the street before darting into a secluded bistro, adrenaline flowing. Rather, once inside, he can focus on the fact that the waiter is both rude and inattentive, the prices are astronomical, and the trendy little portions leave him hungry. Nor will he be forced to come up with intricate excuses about where he was until 3 A.M. Instead, he will be clear-headed enough to start realizing that sex with a twenty-two-year-old may indeed have its moments, but it can also be a bit wearing.

"It was actually kind of amazing," says a thirty-eight-year-old professional chef from New York City.

> From the very day I confronted Ron, he seemed to lose interest in the girl. He reminded me of a big balloon that had just been pricked; right before my eyes, he got smaller and smaller. It may sound strange, but I almost felt sorry for him. He was like a little boy who'd just had a new toy taken away.
>
> I guess I was lucky in the sense that it turned out his affair wasn't exactly an *affair*—it was more of a fling. Our relationship was basically solid, and I think he was only in it for the kicks of being with a twenty-one-year-old, and trying to find ways to sleep with her—the same as he'd done with me when we were both that age. He couldn't go to her apartment because she had three roommates; they couldn't use our apartment, for obvious reasons. So the affair seemed mostly to entail dreaming up adolescent ways to connect in bed. I think sometimes they took the car and drove out to the beach—several times I found sand all over the back seat. And once—Ron told me about this later— he booked a room in a small hotel on the upper west side that a friend of his had recommended. But what he hadn't realized was that it was a residential hotel catering mostly to senior citizens; the friend had neglected to tell him his mother lived there. Ron said that in retrospect it was pretty funny—and pretty sad—sneaking through a lobby filled with wheelchairs and walkers.

While there can be both humor and sadness involved in the aftermath of confrontation, the act itself takes a lot of courage. Coming right out and asking your man if he's having an affair, or telling him you're pretty sure he is, is far from easy. Even if you're 99 percent certain of what he's up to, actually hearing him say the words is enough to shatter even the strongest woman. But think of it this way: If you don't confront him, you're left living a lie. In the end, nobody can tell you what to do, but in our opinion, you almost have to risk confrontation in order for your marriage or relationship to have a chance.

It would be nice if there were one surefire way to confront, but there isn't. In his classic book, *Baby and Child Care,* Benjamin Spock had a wonderful line about the best way to diaper a baby. It depends, said Spock, on the size of the baby and the size of the diaper. The same goes for confrontation: not all men are alike; not all affairs are alike. A partner who's just out for quick sex has to be handled differently from a man who has turned to another woman for the warmth and companionship he hasn't been getting at home. To confront to maximize advantage, then, you have to know your man. Is he earthy or cerebral? Confident or shy? Does he simply need reassurance of your love, or would the shock value of a controlled outburst be more productive? How has he reacted to past confrontations—about money, sharing household tasks, handling the children? Does he tend to become defensive? Does he blow up initially, but then, when the tantrum is over, listen to reason? Your knowledge of his personality, and the way he typically responds, should be a big help in sensing when and how to have your face-off with him. Maybe you should scare him. Demand a retrial. Say absolutely nothing and opt for a physical approach by simply trying to entice him back into your bed. Whatever you do, you should *start him thinking.*

Is it wise to issue an ultimatum—that is, "It's her or me; I'll give you exactly one week (or one day, one hour) to end this affair or it's all over between us"? Understandably, the temptation to do so is strong. Forcing him to choose between you and the other woman right from the start is a way of protecting yourself— you won't have to "humble" yourself by trying to talk him into taking another look at both you and the relationship—and it would seem to offer the bonus of an immediate resolution. That way, he gives her up or he doesn't, you cut off the affair before it has a chance to go any further, and you won't have to suffer through a painful period of uncertainty. Or, he's out the door. At least you'll know where you stand, but the risks are high.

For some women—although we've found them to be in the minority—presenting him with an ultimatum *is* the best approach. But you have to know your man. If ultimatums in any form have always made him stubbornly keep on doing whatever it was that you didn't want him to do, you'll probably be better off not pinning him to the wall right now. If after a reasonable amount of time he hasn't ended the other relationship, you can always give him an ultimatum then. If, on the other hand, he's the sort of person who responds well to clear directives, and only gets confused when presented with options, an ultimatum might indeed work. Try to think it through before you act, though, rather than simply lashing out indiscriminately.

It also isn't a bad idea to have some sense of the competition before you confront—not so you can compare yourself to her but simply to gather more information about what sort of an affair it is. Even if you already have a good idea of why he's doing what he's doing, it never hurts to be even clearer. Ask around a little. Perhaps friends have seen the two of them out together, but haven't dared tell you. Are there any possibilities at his office? It's often surprisingly easy to uncover what you've been determinedly blind to before. You don't want to obsess about her, of course—just see what it is he thinks she offers. Knowing that she's a very young secretary, or a plain but interesting contemporary, or even the sort of woman about whom everybody says, "I can't imagine what he sees in her" is painful, yes, but it will help you be stronger and more focused when you confront. (Don't tell him you know who his girlfriend is; just use the information for your own ends.) And remember—if you can't find out anything about her, it's not a tragedy. By assessing your relationship, and the reason he's strayed, you have more than enough to go on.

Finally, if at all feasible, time your move. It may sound reactionary to advise, "Don't have a knock-down, drag-out discussion when your man really has been working late, and comes home at 10 P.M., cranky and starved." And in a way, it is. But clichés got to be clichés for a reason. It's because over the years, they've proved to be true. (Also, would you want to be confronted about anything when you've just come in from the coast on a plane that was four hours late, and are dying for a drink and a hot bath? It has nothing to do with male or female—just the way people are.) So aim for a moment that seems right; if your antennae are up, you'll know when.

By now, you're probably thinking: "Enough! If he doesn't want me, I don't want him." Okay. Fine. But that's a really limited way of looking at it. Of course, you can toss your head, walk out on what was and probably still is the most important relationship you've ever had, and retain your "pride." But you'll also have given up without even trying. Wouldn't it be better to take pride in fighting for what's rightfully yours? The following five women did just that—and won. All were initially afraid to confront; all had doubts about the final outcome of their relationships. And their feelings of outrage and confusion were every bit as powerful as yours, maybe more so. In retrospect, however, all say if they hadn't dared to confront their men, they would have felt even more degraded. Why? Because doing nothing would have been tantamount to saying the relationship meant nothing— that *they* meant nothing. There's no particular honor in defeat; by putting their hearts on the line, they acted. And with action came the first step toward control—not of him, not of the relationship, but of their own lives. Perhaps hearing their stories will help you say yes to confrontation, and decide how best to do it.

I'd suspected for quite a while that he was up to something, but I thought it was just a meaningless little fling, so I gritted my teeth and ignored what was going on—although I was absolutely seething inside. He did all the usual—lots of "late nights" at the office, sneaking in at four in the morning, picking fights over nothing, no interest in sex. He had a way of not looking at me that made me want to die. Anyway, one evening—I remember it so vividly it seems like yesterday—I went into the bedroom, and he was sitting there, slumped over, his head in his hands. At that moment he looked so miserable, so vulnerable, I just blurted it out: "You're having an affair, aren't you?" God, it was awful. Awful. He began to cry— said he was pulled to pieces, all the lying and sneaking around, that I deserved better than that. He told me he still loved me, but he was also in love with someone else, a woman he worked with, and he wanted a divorce—it seemed the only way. He even told me she'd said if he didn't get one, she'd leave him; she couldn't take it anymore. She couldn't take it!

My first instinct was to cave in, to say, "all right; if that's what you want, go ahead." But from somewhere—it was as if I were standing outside myself, listening—I heard myself telling him I would never give him a divorce, that I cared too much about us, about him, about our marriage. I think that was the last response he expected—you've never seen a man look so stunned. Maybe he hadn't realized I cared that much. Or maybe he'd thought all he had to do was ask for a divorce and I'd give it to him. Well, he sure found out differently.

—Terry, editor, age forty-six

We were in bed. By then, our sex life was almost non-existent—we hadn't made love in over three months, and of course I knew why; he'd been with her. I planned it all very carefully. I was wearing this sexy black lace teddy, no panties, I'd just showered, the sheets were clean. His back was to me, as usual, but I swallowed all pride and just started touching him . . . slowly, slowly. When he was really turned on, I whispered: "Can she do this? Can she make you feel this good?" After that, he knew that I knew. And that was the beginning of the end of her.

—Denise, assistant art director, age twenty-eight

I confronted the two of them in person. Outrageous? I guess so, but I'd reached the stage where I was either going to make a flamboyant, go-for-broke gesture or just pack it in. Maybe if I'd spoken up earlier I wouldn't have had to resort to such a tactic, but I was so hurt, so angry, I wasn't thinking very clearly. I knew who she was and where she lived, so one night, when I was pretty certain he was with her, I drove over and rang the bell. When she answered, I yelled that I knew he was in there, and she'd better let me in. I heard her call out to him, and then I could hear them talking, although I couldn't make out the words. Finally, she opened the door, and my husband was standing behind her, a ham and cheese sandwich in one hand. The sight of that sandwich made me livid—it reminded me of all the nights I'd come home from work and fixed a nice dinner, only to have him show up three hours late and say he wasn't hungry—he'd had a hamburger at his desk. Well, it was too much. I lunged at her, screaming that he was my husband, and he was coming home with me this minute— one word out of her and I'd kill her. I was actually holding onto the neck of her sweater, shaking her back and forth, as I said this—me, the sort of person who never, ever, raises her voice. While this sweet little scene was going on, my husabnd just stood there, looking first at me, then at her. He didn't seem able to believe what was happening. It wasn't until she began screaming for help that he suddenly came out of his trance, pried me off her, and hurried me out the door. Maybe he was afraid I really would kill her. Anyway, once I told him how hurt and furious I was, he didn't seem as interested in seeing her. I think he was flattered—forty-five years old and two women fighting over him. I'm not saying this is the best way to go about confronting; it's just the way it happened.

—Lauren, public relations representative, age forty-one

I didn't ask him, I told him—which at the time took a lot of chutzpah because in fact, I wasn't absolutely certain. But from the moment he thought I knew about the other woman, everything came out; it was as if I'd unleashed a floodgate. He kept begging me to forgive him——it didn't mean anything, he said; she'd just been there, been available, and in the beginning it had made him feel good, knowing that another woman thought he was so hot and sexy. But now he was going crazy——she was making all these demands, threatening to tell me, calling him at work every half hour.

He didn't know what to do; it was all too much for him. At one point, he even asked me what he should do. I listened to this outpouring in total shock, but finally collected myself enough to tell him that he was to call the woman now and inform her his wife knew all about the affair, and that she was never to call or try to see him again. It was over. Then, while he was on the phone with her, I went into the bathroom and threw up.

——Susan, co-owner of a boutique, age thirty-six

I told him I knew exactly what he was doing, and that he couldn't come back home until it was over. In other words, I basically threw him out. That really shocked him——he hadn't even been aware that I knew anything about the affair. I stood over him while he packed a bag——it was a very small bag, by the way, which seemed a good sign——and the whole time he kept saying that maybe we should talk about it; breaking up was a big step. But I was a stone——wouldn't budge an inch. When the door shut, I leaned against it, shaking, for what seemed like forever. But I knew instinctively that I'd done the right thing. Call me old-fashioned, but I couldn't live in the same house with a man who was unfaithful. It had to be her or me.

——Justine, travel agent, age thirty-three

It would obviously be silly to say: Do as these women did and your life will immediately return to normal (or better than normal), so we won't say it. All of life's a gamble, and you never know. But it *is* a fact that in your quest to get your man back, having the courage to confront is a major asset . . . and it's not the only one.

CHAPTER 5

You've Got The Power!

But enough about him—what about you? Right now, you have to make the most important decision among all of those that lie ahead. *You have to choose yourself over him.* Why? Because, ultimately, this is the only way to get him back, and what is even more important, it's the only way to stay sane. Nobody is a higher priority than you are at the moment. Nobody! We're not saying you should neglect the kids, or wrap yourself in a cocoon of selfishness that shuts everyone else out—quite the contrary. What we are saying is that you must be good to yourself, pamper yourself, appreciate yourself as never before. What Mildred Newman and Bernard Berkowitz talked about in their classic bestseller, *How to Be Your Own Best Friend,* still holds— you *can* be your own best friend, and we're going to help you learn how to get the most out of that friendship.

Definitely, making a concentrated effort to regain your sense of self—and self-worth—is the single most positive action you can take at this point. Yet refusing to let outside forces wobble the ego can be a tough problem for women, even in the best of times—and this isn't one of the best times. So exactly what, you might wonder, are you supposed to do? You're supposed to cope, that's what. And you're going to do it by telling yourself you have to get through this, you will get through this, and that you'll unquestionably wind up a stronger, more productive woman for having done so. The following tactics will help ease the coping process, making you feel better and more together sooner than you'd ever have thought possible.

REACH OUT

Remember when you were a little girl, and you'd run to Mom whenever you scraped your knee so she could make it better? Well, what you need now is the same kind of comfort and support you got from Mom, but you need it from insightful, compassionate contemporaries who also have your best interests at heart. Remind yourself that there's nothing to be ashamed of in asking for help—you're living through a crisis, and are smart enough to know you have to do something about it. Far from being a sign of weakness, reaching out shows that you're strong.

If you don't succeed the first—or even second or third—time you reach out, take a deep breath and force yourself to keep on reaching. (Not easy when you're feeling so vulnerable, we know, but it shows you're even stronger.) Some women have got themselves into pretty gruesome tangles when they first started looking for help—the shrink, the friend, the family member they were certain they could count on turned out to be anything but supportive. Let's hope this doesn't happen to you, but if it does, the important thing is not to give up. Good people *are* out there . . . and with a little courage (and luck), you'll find them. Listen to Marie, a forty-eight-year-old freelance writer from New York City:

When Larry said he wanted a divorce, I was so shocked that I insisted on going to his shrink with him. He'd been seeing the man for over a year, but I'd never before demanded to sit in on a session. The shrink, one of the most loathsome human beings I've ever met in my life, immediately told me I'd been a terrible wife to Larry, and that his impotence was all my fault—no wonder he'd turned to another woman for comfort. He also said that I was just generally a pretty terrible person, like many wives he'd known. Throughout it all, Larry just sat there, smirking. I could sort of understand Larry's behavior, but I simply couldn't believe a psychiatrist, and a well-known one, at that, would say such things. In a way, it snapped me out of my stunned state.

"Well!" I said. "Since I'm so terrible, do you think there's any hope for me, or should I end it all now?" I was kidding, but not that much.

"That's for you to decide," he said, dead seriously. But he was magnanimous enough to add that I should definitely see a female therapist—assuming I decided to live—and promised to get me a name by the end of the week. He didn't say *why* he thought it was so important I see a woman—it sounded kind of sexist and fishy to me—but at that point, I was in no shape to argue.

The end of the week came, and he called and said he hadn't been able to find a woman for me after all; he did, however, give me the name of a male colleague of his. Since by now I was determined to play the whole thing out, I went to see the doctor he'd recommended. Well, I didn't like *him* one bit, either. He was very dour and Freudian. I expected him to be as outraged as I about the way Larry's shrink had treated me, but when I told him what had happened, all he said was, "Hmm." Anyway, when the session was over, I knew I didn't want to go back to him or *anyone* associated with that first doctor, and I told him so—which made me feel great. This shrink did offer me what turned out to be a lifesaving piece of advice, though. "There's a divorce therapy group starting at the YMHA on

Ninety-Second Street in the next week or two," he said. "I suggest you sign up." "But I don't want a divorce!" I said, indignantly. Still, I was desperate, so I went to the Y, and at a total cost of about eighty-five dollars, I spent two hours a week for the next eight weeks in the most helpful therapy I've ever had. I couldn't believe a seemingly stuffy old Freudian had recommended it. There were fifteen of us—men and women, young and not-so-young. Some had been divorced for over a year; others were in the midst of painful breakups; still others, like myself, were simply in troubled marriages. I'd never had much confidence in the idea of group therapy before, but I was wrong. Just talking to sympathetic people in similar situations helped me enormously. Two counselors ran the group, but they didn't say much. Mostly, we helped each other, and that help got me through the toughest part—the stage when Larry wanted a divorce.

Get this, though. Larry finally decided he didn't want a divorce after all; he realized another woman wouldn't solve his problems. What happened was that once the other woman business was out in the open, Larry and I started talking to each other as we never had before. He told me he'd been feeling frozen out by me in the marriage—said I'd always seemed so busy with my deadlines and the kids, he'd begun to feel he wasn't important to me anymore. And I had to face up to the fact that in many ways he was right. Sometimes, when I'd been late with a magazine article, and trying to cope with our sixteen-year-old—who'd decided to go on a homework sabbatical—I'd just turn into a screaming crazy. I'd been venting most of my frustrations on Larry, and this had taken a toll on our sex life—which hadn't been great for a long time, anyway. I realized I'd been so distracted I hadn't paid any attention to what Larry needed, and when I finally saw that, I was able to do something about it.

Larry confessed that he'd never been in love with this other woman—she'd simply been a pleasant diversion when things were tense at home. So we decided to concentrate on each other for a change, and make a real effort to keep our marriage together.

When he explained this to his shrink, the awful man said, "Then get out of my office—and don't bother to come back." Can you believe it? Frankly, I think that doctor is more screwed up than either Larry or I have ever been. It just goes to show that you have to be careful about whom you decide to trust—and that the title "psychiatrist" doesn't necessarily mean you'll get top-level help.

Marie was lucky on two counts. First, she trusted her instincts on whether or not someone was the right therapist for her, and second, she learned almost by accident about a valuable source of help. Here are some ways for you to uncover sources that may not previously have occurred to you:

1. CALL FRIENDS AND FAMILY

Ask whom they know who's gotten help that really worked. You'll be surprised at how many good counselors there are, and at how many people you know are going to them.

Not everyone necessarily needs or wants professional help, of course, but for most of the women we talked with, it was invaluable. If you don't feel you'd get anything out of therapy, you could be right, but we strongly suggest you at least give it a try. A skilled, sympathetic therapist may have insights you never dreamed of, and is invariably able to help short-circuit much pain and anxiety. Also, most professionals set their fees on a sliding scale, so don't let money worries slow you down. Just keep looking and asking until you find someone you like and and trust.

2. CALL YOUR CHURCH OR SYNAGOGUE

Make an appointment with your minister, priest, or rabbi. If you'd prefer, simply explain your situation to someone in the administration office, and ask if there's a person or organization to which they can refer you.

3. CALL YOUR LOCAL HOSPITALS

Again, explain your problem and ask if they have a referral service or can suggest a doctor or counselor for you to get in touch with.

4. CALL NEARBY COLLEGES AND UNIVERSITIES

Sometimes, colleges have very sophisticated counseling set-ups. Even if they don't, they can probably tell you where else to call for information.

5. CALL YOUR LOCAL YMCA, YWCA AND YMHA

If counseling programs aren't available, these organizations, too, should be able to tell you where to call.

6. CALL YOUR OWN DOCTOR

He or she is often the best person to put you in touch with an appropriate therapist, or to suggest where to go for professional group therapy.

7. LOOK IN THE YELLOW PAGES

Sounds a little ridiculous at first, right? Why should you—a sophisticated, aware woman with a slew of friends to offer recommendations and advice, even a cousin who's a counselor herself—start going through the *phone book?* Well, maybe because you aren't ready to talk to friends and relatives about your situation just yet, and would rather look for help on your own. (It can be both embarrassing and upsetting to let the entire world in on the fact that your man is running around with someone else, and lots of women would rather keep it to themselves.) One of the most obvious sources of that help is often overlooked: the good old Yellow Pages. Check the index under:

- Clinics
- Counselors
- Divorce counseling
- Family counseling
- Marriage counseling
- Individual counseling
- Meditation services
- Psychologists
- Social and human services
- Social workers

After you've called and connected with a service that sounds good to you, check it out; ask for references and call them. And remember Marie's experience—trust your instincts. If, for any reason, you don't like the person or place you've seen, whatever his or her credentials, don't go back—that little inner voice you've been learning to listen to is probably absolutely right. Any counselor or group that makes you uncomfortable—even if it's just the way a therapist refuses to look you in the eye, or the fact that group members ramble on about "sharing," and "inner environments"—isn't going to work, so keep on looking. When you *do* find the right sort of help for you, you'll know.

If you've already tried out the above suggestions and had no luck, then take a close look at the groups and associations listed in the Appendix. All either offer help for women in troubled marriages—in some cases, with those needing advice on, or support during, divorce—or will make referrals.

COMPARTMENTALIZE

Okay, let's assume you've taken the first positive step. You've found—or are on your way to finding—good, objective help. What else can you do for yourself? Plenty.

To begin with, it's important to accept that all those feelings of self-doubt swirling around in your head are perfectly normal. In an August 1991 *Cosmo* article called "Self-esteem; You Can Have It (Almost) All the Time," Cambridge, Massachusetts, psychologist Susan Schenkel put it this way: "Loss of love is a blow to anyone's sense of self, and it's terribly misleading of certain self-help books to imply that there's something wrong with women whose sense of themselves is shaken by the disintegration of a serious love relationship. I'd be a lot more worried about anyone—male or female—who felt wonderful in those circumstances." So, whatever you do, don't start to punish yourself for punishing yourself—if you know what we mean. Many old insecurities you thought you'd put to rest years ago may start to crop up now, so just accept this, and do your best to keep on going.

One way to get yourself through the worst of the doubting period is to compartmentalize, New York City psychologist JoAnn Magdoff suggested in the same *Cosmo* article. She pointed out that a woman's sense of self-worth resides in many compartments—intelligence, appearance, competence, love, sex, and work are only a few. When one area is threatened, the healthy thing to do, said Magdoff, is to throw yourself into another. So when your husband or lover is temporarily out of the picture, you might try to compensate by concentrating on your career (volunteer work counts, too), or even letting yourself get a little obsessive about a hobby—photography, say, or refinishing furniture—or maybe developing a talent you'd forgotten you had, like painting. Whatever it is, try to lead with your strong suit. "It doesn't make you feel less damaged as a love object to know that you can perform well at work or be a good mother or friend, but it does remind you that there are undamaged parts of your psyche," Magdoff noted. "And that's a very useful reminder while you're trying to rebuild the self-esteem that's been eroded by a bad end to a relationship."

Magdoff's advice is just as sound for those who aren't sure what the outcome of the relationship is going to be, but are having to make some tough adjustments at the moment. Compartmentalizing won't eradicate pain and self-doubt but it will certainly help hold them at bay.

GET UPBEAT

We are what we think. Simple, isn't it? But have you ever stopped to consider just how true it is? We all have friends who aren't particularly attractive or gifted, but for whom everything seems to go right. They have adoring husbands, play the best tennis game in town, always seem to be surrounded by loving friends and family. Then we have other friends who have much more going for them in terms of looks, talent, brains, or wit but who somehow never seem to get the man, job, or invitation they were hoping for. Why? Because the first batch of women believe they *deserve* to have what they want . . . and those in the second group don't.

Nothing, nothing, nothing is more destructive than telling yourself, "Of course, he left me. I'm too fat," or "I'd love to apply for that reporting job on the local newspaper, but they'd never dream of hiring anyone as shy and insecure as I am." Why *do* you keep sending yourself these negative messages? What's in it for you?

Let's take the fat issue as an example. Maybe you have gained weight lately, and aren't happy about it. But do you really believe that having put on some extra pounds is an act so terrible it warrants losing a husband? Come on! You're a deserving person whether you weigh 105 or 175. If being overweight makes *you* unhappy, then make up your mind to go on a diet and get back to the weight you feel and look best at, but don't for a second think you're unworthy or undesirable just because you don't have the figure of a sylph. Putting yourself down may *seem* like a form of self-protection (i.e., if I'm fat, no man can ever hurt me again because no man will come near me), but in fact, this sort of reasoning guarantees misery. There's nothing wrong with trying to lose weight, but weight *per se* has nothing to do with it. Accepting yourself, and taking charge of your life, does.

If you let the negative feelings about yourself stop you from improving other areas of your life, you will only feel more depressed. If you tell yourself, for instance, that you're too much of a wimp to have a chance of getting that job on a local paper, and therefore don't even bother to send in a résumé or call for an appointment, you've saved yourself the pain of possible rejection, yes, but you've also denied yourself the opportunity to do work you'd really enjoy. Not only that, you've reinforced those nagging little fears about not being worth much, anyway. Instead, simply say, "Well, I may not get the job, but I think I'll go for an interview and find out what it's all about." You may not get the job, but the person doing the hiring may suggest another opening—maybe something you'd like even more. He or she may offer you a freelance assignment, or recommend you to a colleague on another paper, or just give you some valuable advice. The worst scenario would be that nothing happens at all, but even then, we promise you'll feel better about yourself for having tried.

For many women, negative thinking is just an old habit—and like any habit, it's tough to break. But break it you must, if you're going to prevail in your attempt to get what you need. Whenever you're tempted to send yourself a negative message, ask why you're doing it. Are you trying to protect yourself from any sort of risk that might lead to rejection? Curling up in a comfortable (because it's familiar) cocoon of self-pity? What are you *really* after? Think it through. Then maybe you'll see that it's time to appreciate all the marvelous qualities you do have to offer, and get on with it.

Try this. The next time you feel one of those tenacious, negative old thoughts creeping up on you, as in—"If Larry doesn't move back, I just know I'll never be able to attract another man"— say "Stop/Switch." *Stop* that downbeat, ridiculous idea and *switch* another, positive one for it. You might substitute something like, "I'm smart and funny and good-hearted—there are lots of men who'd appreciate these qualities." Or, how about the following Stop/Switches?:

Thought: "I'm always so depressed, it's no wonder people don't like to be around me."

Stop/Switch: "Of course I'm depressed right now—who wouldn't be?—and I have many wonderful friends who understand."

Thought: "Maybe if I'd been a little more passive and docile, he would have stayed."

Stop/Switch: "It's okay to be strong and independent, and if he left because I'm not a marshmallow, maybe I'd better think about whether I really want him back."

Thought: "If only I had Kathleen Turner's legs, I'd be just fine."

Stop/Switch: "Only Kathleen Turner has Kathleen Turner's legs. My legs are just fine. My figure is just fine. I'm just fine."

The Stop/Switch method can also be used to push out negative thoughts that have been swirling around since early childhood or teen years, and do nothing to further a sturdy self-image, either. Stop/Switch helps you stop blaming Mom and Dad, or sneaky little Suzie Rittenhouse—who, in first grade, whispered that your nose looked like Pinocchio's—for all your image problems. Here, two telling examples:

Thought: "I'd feel a lot better about myself if my father had told me, even once, that I was pretty."

Stop/Switch: "Naturally, it would have been nice if Dad had said I was the prettiest little girl ever, but he was probably only doing what every other father on the block was doing at that point in time—trying to make sure his kid didn't get a swelled head."

Thought: "I wouldn't be so insecure and self-effacing if my mother hadn't had a drinking problem. With her, I never knew where I stood."

Stop/Switch: "I can have compassion for my mother, feel sorrow for a childhood that was lacking in the stability all children crave, and still refuse to let that childhood affect me *now*. As a grown-up, I am responsible for my own happiness and sense of worth."

Stop/Switch works. The technique may sound a little basic, but actually, it's one of the fundamental principles of cognitive therapy. You really can learn to control and reprogram negative thought patterns, so, for the next twenty-four hours, use Stop/Switch every time one of those gloomy, self-deprecating thoughts crops up. You'll feel as if you're playing a game at first, but after a while, you'll get more comfortable with it. It is the cornerstone of empowerment—tell yourself you can and you *can*. Call it the power of positive thinking, call it thought control, call it Learned Optimism, as Martin Seligman does in his lucid new book of the same title,—call it whatever you like. Teaching yourself to erase the negative and concentrate on the positive will give you more control over your life, more peace of mind, than you've ever had before.

Right now, are you saying, "Yeah, sure, but this will never work for me?" Stop/Switch.

TAKE ACTION—TEN TOP TO-DO'S

Now that you've given your way of thinking a major overhaul, it's time to get behind the wheel and start moving. The following is a list of what we call the *To-Do's,* the ten most important steps you can take to get yourself back on track to security, self-esteem, and just plain fun!

START TALKING

No, we don't mean to the carrots in the supermarket, or to David Letterman on *Late Night;* we mean to those real live people all around you. Chat with the person who puts gas in your car, talk to the nice lady at the dry cleaners, call up old college chums. Why all this verbal action? For two reasons. First, because what you need now are connections—new people to get involved with, no matter how superficial the contact. Since there *is* this temporary void in your life, you want to fill it quickly, not necessarily with a new man—although some women find a little judicious intrigue doesn't hurt—but with everyone in your world. Given the slightest encouragement, many of them will show you how concerned and supportive they can be.

The second reason to start talking is that you'll be amazed at how charming and effective you can be. You may not end up being best friends with the man at the gas station, but you sure may get a better lube job next time around.

START LISTENING

Of course, you're distracted; of course, you sometimes have a hard time concentrating. But do yourself—and the people in your life—the favor of really listening; few actions will serve you better. When your son says he's having a terrible time with his algebra, don't just brush it off with an "I'm sure you'll do fine, dear." Instead, get him to talk about it. Have him explain just what it is that's so difficult for him. (And, unless you happen to have a Ph.D. in nuclear physics, also help him to figure out how to get the most effective tutoring.) When your best friend calls the same morning she has to have two wisdom teeth pulled, hear her out and sympathize. Yes, you've got problems too, but the wisdom-tooth stuff is no picnic, and focusing on her woes for a few minutes will help you forget your own. When the taxi driver says, "I hate this town and I gotta get out of here before I explode, listen (unless you sense he may be a true crazy, in which case, pretend you speak only French). When you take them and their problems seriously, people know. They appreciate it. They value you because of it. And before long, you'll be getting back just as much (maybe even more) as you're giving. Listening is loving—sounds sappy, maybe, but it's the truth. Try it. You'll like yourself better, and everybody else will, too.

INVEST IN YOUR APPEARANCE

A while back, we said "fat has nothing to do with it," and it doesn't. Your man didn't leave because you were too fat, or too tall, or too anything. He left for his own, probably neurotic reasons, which we've already gone into. But it's also true that for most of us, looking good plays a big part in feeling good. Nobody is going to expect you to have Madonna's body, Meryl Streep's cheekbones, and Kim Bassinger's mouth, and you shouldn't expect it of yourself, either. On the other hand, there's no reason not to make the most of what you have for your own sense of well-being—not because you're trying to compete. So select what appeals to you from the following suggestions and go for it.!

Haircut. Easy, painless, and usually 100 percent effective in boosting morale. Either check in with your stylist and explain that you want something wild and wonderful and different, or do a little research. Get recommendations from soignée friends; if you see a woman on the street whose hair you like, ask her who did it. (Don't be shy—she's bound to be flattered.) You might want to consider color, too: Get rid of that gray or brighten up that brunette. Highlights are another option. Don't try any radical color shifts right now—going from dark brown, say, to platinum. Not only are the odds heavy that the new shade will be wrong for your skin tone, such a big switch makes it seem you're trying too hard. A subtle change is all you need.

Manicure. Quick, inexpensive, makes you feel pampered. These days, for between five and ten dollars, you can get a walk-in, professional manicure just about anywhere in the country. Why not treat yourself once a week?

Diet. "Oh, *no!*" you say. "It's too hard for me to lose weight. Nothing ever works." Well, if that's the case, it's because you've never really made up your mind to take it off and keep it off. Until you decide you are absolutely, positively going to lose ten (or twenty, even thirty) pounds, nothing's going to happen. But once you're determined, you'll do it. Willpower is all. We talked with a woman who'd put on forty-five pounds in the ten years she'd been married; after her husband left, she drew up a plan: Says Amy:

> I decided to wait until January, as it's always tough to diet over the holidays. But I promised myself that I'd lose twenty pounds in six months, starting the first of the year. I was afraid I wouldn't have enough willpower on my own, so I joined Weight Watchers, and week after week, the pounds kept coming off. My friends were amazed. So was my husband, who was then living with the girlfriend—I refused to acknowledge that she had a name, and just called her "the girlfriend." Anyway, I felt terrific, not simply because I looked so much better, but because I'd had the discipline to actually do this for myself. It's been two years now— the girlfriend is history, incidentally—and I haven't gained back a single pound. What I loved most about losing was that it showed me I could take charge of my life. Sam's coming home was just a part of all that. . . .

Exercise.   Nobody's suggesting you start running ten miles a day, or begin training for the Olympic squash team, but you'll feel so much better when your body's in good shape. You'll sleep better, have more energy, be more productive, better able to relax. Also, exercise is the best natural enemy of depression. Study after study has shown that when you exercise regularly and consistently, in a way that keeps your heart rate slightly elevated for at least twenty minutes, magical little endorphins are released in the brain. These natural proteins have potent analgesic properties that give you a sort of natural high, a soothing sense of well-being, and the cozy feeling that everything's going to be okay.

Whatever exercises you decide to do, regularity is the key— at least twenty minutes, three times a week. Whether it's fifty jumps with the jump rope or just jogging in place, set a modest goal for yourself and keep to it, adding to your program as stamina increases. You should start noticing a difference after the first week. Here, a rundown on some of the most popular types of exercise:

1. Aerobics.   You can do these at home alone—perhaps with the help of one of the dozens of videos on the market— or in a class (a great place to meet new people). Make sure you don't try to do too much too soon; pulled ligaments and sprained ankles are not the goal. Low-impact aerobics and step-aerobics are both very popular right now, and for good reason—they're safer.

2. Yoga.   Many people swear by this gentle, relaxing, meditative form of exercise. Even if you're following a more "physical" exercise program, yoga can be a valuable supplement. Bonus: It revitalizes mind as well as body.

3. Weight Training.   This includes working out with all those fancy Nautilus machines, exercise bikes, rowing machines, treadmills, as well as free weights. Virtually every health club offers such training. You'll need help at the beginning, so you can learn to pace yourself and operate the machines properly. Once you're proficient, you might also want to invest in your own exercise bike or treadmill.

4. Dancercise.   Jazz, tap, modern . . . any kind of dance class provides fabulous exercise. Not only does your body get a great workout, but the artistic, expressive part of you is allowed free rein, too. If you have kids, you might want to take them with you. Children love to dance, and lots of Y's have mother/ child classes that end up being fun (and funny) as well as figure-enhancing.

5. Calisthenics.   A little rigorous for some of us, maybe, but a good, quick-result-producing form of exercise. Some instruction is required at first, but once you're worked out a suitable routine, you can do it anywhere—well, almost anywhere.

6. *Walking*.   It's the simplest, most effortless, and—according to many experts—best type of exercise. The beauty of walking is that you can fit it into your regular daily routine. Walk to the office each morning, or for a mile or two before you go to work. The important thing here is to keep up a brisk pace— we're talking about real walking, not sauntering—and to walk for twenty minutes or more. It is the favorite exercise of models— they don't want to develop muscles, just to stay trim and toned. Not a bad idea for all of us. And walking is free.

7. *Sports*.   Then there are the naturals—swimming, biking, golf, tennis, squash, bowling, hiking, skiing, paddle tennis— anything that gets you moving fast and concentrating hard. If you used to be on the swim team in high school, or were a major cross-country skier but gave it up when the kids came along— *un*give it up! Go back to your former sport, or be bold and take up a new one. You'll be surprised at how much encouragement you'll get and how eager friends—old and new—will be to help you along.

8. *Cosmetic surgery*.   Some women believe aging gracefully is beautiful—and if that's how you feel, fine. But assuming you don't—if puffy eyes, sagging breasts, age spots or anything else bothers you—then do something about it. Just be sure to choose a highly recommended, board-certified surgeon, and make certain you feel comfortable with him or her. If a little tuck or tightening will make you feel better about your appearance, then we're all for it. Do remember to ask the doctor exactly what the procedure involves, how long it will take to recover, and how much it will cost; only when you have all the facts can you make a valid decision.

If you're not interested in anything as radical as surgery, you might check in with your dermatologist and find out what's new in the collagen department. Lots of women have regular injections of one of this substances, and swear by it. The procedure is far cheaper than surgery, and according to devotees, makes a world of difference in looks. Judging by recent reports, silicone is a no-no.

BRUSH UP YOUR SKILLS

We're not talking about taking a typing course; we're talking about getting back in touch with the interests and talents that used to give you so much pleasure. Maybe gardening was your forte, but you've let it slide. Or maybe you once adored writing poetry. Whatever your special gift, now's the time to develop it. One woman we spoke with had been a photojournalist when she first got out of college, but hadn't held a camera in years. When her husband announced he was moving in with a thirty-one-year-old colleague, she instinctively turned to the avocation that had once been so gratifying.

"I decided to sign up for a course in black and white photography, at an art school in town," Liz said.

> Initially, I was terrified I'd be at least twenty years older than anyone else, and that I'd seem like a real dunce—so much has changed in photography since I was involved with it. But my fears were for nothing. There were two people about my age in the class, and I've become great friends with one of them. He works for the local newspaper, is getting divorced, and we often spend weekend afternoons taking pictures together. He's helped me to get excited about my work again, which has been a lifesaver for me. As for knowing less than the younger students—well, it was true when it came to equipment, but I was surprised to find out that I was just as talented as most of the kids. And anyway, what really mattered was getting back into the field I loved so much.

Whatever talents or interests you harbor, nurture them. At the moment, you have a unique opportunity to get to know yourself, to cultivate your own garden as well as the one in the back yard, if that's one of your passions.

LEAN A LITTLE

As we've said, there's absolutely nothing wrong with asking for help when you're going through a tough time, so don't be shy about calling a good friend and telling her you need her sympathetic ear over dinner (your treat), or asking that fun Maine cousin if you could come up for a weekend to lick your wounds. Shrinks aren't the only ones to reach out to—there are lots of people in your life who care about you and want to see you happy. Use them.

Make new friends, too. Aside from just talking to the world at large, zero in on people you think would be compatible, and really extend yourself—go out of your way to be friendly. Swallow that fear of rejection—"Oh, she'd never want to have lunch with *me*"—and get to know some of the lively, interesting people you've haven't paid much attention to before. Ask that charming neighbor over for coffee. Organize after-work drinks with the singles at your office; throw out feelers to the marrieds about having a meal or seeing a movie, when their husbands are otherwise occupied. You may have a few disappointments, but most of the time, people will respond positively, and life will start to open up as never before.

"I was so nervous about asking the art director if she'd like to go shopping with me some day at lunch that I put it off for weeks," one forty-five-year-old advertising copywriter told us.

> I'd always liked Sally, but she seemed so busy and important, and obviously, I was feeling more fragile than usual. What woman who's recently discovered her husband is having an affair wouldn't? So I was really worried about getting turned down. Well, I finally suggested it, and she was thrilled— said there was a sale at Sak's she'd been dying to go to. After shopping, we had a quick sandwich, and she told me all about her family, and how hard it was for her to commute into the city from the suburbs, leaving two small children with a housekeeper. We're close friends now and see a lot

of each other. I've even visited Sally and her husband at their house a few times.

I can't tell you how glad I am that I forced myself to approach Sally. I'd had a good feeling about her all along, and now that we're friends, she's been wonderfully supportive. I think you have to trust your instincts—when someone appeals to you, you should push yourself to get to know them. The good feelings are almost always mutual, and the emotional payoff is enormous.

Tip: Stay away from downbeat people—the last thing you need right now is negative-think. If you suspect someone has hostile, destructive ways of looking at the world, even if they're on your side (i.e., "I'm not surprised he ran off with that bimbo," or "All men are animals,") dump that person—at least for now. This doesn't mean you'll have to give up valued friends forever, but if they're rigid in their negativism (they may have other sterling qualities), then let them be. When you're feeling stronger and more resilient, you can pick up these old friendships again. At present, however, survival is paramount—yours, that is.

LIVE A LITTLE

This is the time in your life when it's essential to try new things. Always been terrified of roller coasters? Ride one. Think swimming is great for dolphins but you're afraid to put your face under water? Take swimming lessons. Shy about initiating social activities? Buy two tickets to the symphony and invite someone to go with you. Nervous in groups? Organize a neighborhood barbecue and ask each neighbor to contribute (this last may be a little ambitious, but you get the idea).

Francis, a fifty-two-year-old wife and mother, even decided to travel around Europe by herself after her husband left:

I was pretty nervous at first, but I knew it would only be for two weeks, so every morning, I made myself get up and see everything there was to see. The hardest part was having dinner alone, but there were many times when people I'd met in museums, or while having a cappuccino in a piazza, would ask me to join them for a meal.

The high point was in Florence, where I met a darling German man who took me out dancing one night. Me, *dancing!* I just couldn't believe it. There was absolutely nothing complicated about our time together. We were just having fun—I'd almost forgotten what it was like to have a good time. Best of all, Jack—that's my husband—and his girlfriend hardly ever crossed my mind. Also, both kids were away working at summer jobs, and I knew they were safe and busy, so I hardly ever thought about them, either.

What that trip did for me was marvelous. For the first time in years, I was really myself, without all the labels of wife, mother, great soufflé cook. The same problems were still there when I got home, but I felt differently about them. I knew I was going to be okay, no matter what happened with Jack. Ironically, while I was gone, he decided he'd made a terrible mistake and wanted to come back. But I've taken a wait-and-see position. It may all work out in the end, but at the moment, I'm loving my freedom, and I'm in no hurry to pick up old roles again. I think those two weeks alone in France and Italy did more for me than two years of psychoanalysis would have done. My advice? Beg, save, or borrow the money, do whatever you have to, but change your environment for a while. Getting away gives you a whole new perspective—helps you see how lucky you are in a lot of ways—and, most important, shows you that you can rely on yourself, and enjoy it.

A trip to Europe may not be the answer for you, but maybe learning to drive a car is. Whatever the impulse, indulge it; swallow the fear and press on. Even something as simple as going to a movie by yourself (as long as it's not a sad one) can make a difference. Just decide on, say, three things you'd like to do and do them. Then do them again. It gets easier and more fun each time.

LAUGH A LITTLE

Even when life is going well, it's often hard to find situations and people who make you laugh, and this certainly couldn't be classified as a prime period. Nevertheless, do make an effort to expose yourself to amusing people, funny films, witty books, anything that will bring a smile to your face. Studies show that laughter *heals;* it soothes and calms, simply feels good.

You'll know best what tickles your funnybone, but books by Dave Barry, Irma Bombeck, Cynthia Heimel, Wendy Wasserstein, Alice Kahn, Nora Ephron, Russell Baker, Judith Viorst, and Linda Sunshine almost guarantee giggles. On TV, "Cheers," "Saturday Night Live," and "I Love Lucy" reruns are just a few of the shows that should do the trick. And don't overlook old movies such as the vintage Woody Allen's, the Pink Panther series, classics like *Bringing Up Baby*.

Best of all, though, is to surround yourself with (or at least connect with one or two) funny people. Whether it's the clerk at the hardware store or a colleague at work, hang out as much as you can with those who make you laugh. If children and animals get you going, borrow a friend's toddler for the afternoon and spend an hour at the zoo, watching the seals act silly. Think back to *anything* that used to start you chuckling, and seek it out. That may sound as if we're asking you to smile through your tears, but, hey—what's so bad about that?

LOVE A LITTLE

We're not talking about romantic love here; what we *are* talking about is love of life, what the French call *joie de vivre*—the ability to take pleasure in everything from other people to activities to just smelling the roses. Of course, there are going to be times when you don't even want to get out of bed (though we hope you're past most of that by now). But open yourself up to what's going on around you—even once—and you'll see that the rewards are so immediate and great, you won't want to stop. Does music make you come alive? Well, why not see if there are any local singing groups you can join? Or, march yourself down to the nearest church or synagogue (even if you haven't been inside one in years) and see about joining the choir. Does politics make you feel plugged in? Volunteer to work for your favorite candidate!

You might also consider adopting a puppy or kitten—many of the women we spoke with did just that. You'll get lots of satisfying strokes, and caring for your new roomie can be almost a full-time commitment—which may well provide the distraction you need right now. So what if it's not as glamorous as a night at the opera—you're *loving,* aren't you?

We've been talking a lot about how to increase self-esteem, but did you know that one of the best ways to do so is to nurture the egos of others? When a friend is depressed because she didn't get the job she wanted, help her see that she's terrific anyway, and that maybe it wasn't such a great job for her in the first place. You'll both feel better, and, that's what loving a little is all about.

Loving life isn't easy when it has so recently hurt you. But you have to muster up all your willpower and courage, and try. Loosen up, lighten up, leave those poor-me feelings behind. There's a lot of love locked up inside you, and the more you let it out, the happier and healthier you'll be.

In her book *Revolution From Within,* Gloria Steinem puts it this way: "As wise men and women in every culture tell us, the art of life is using whatever happens." So, use it. Turn this traumatic time into a terrific time—well, at least an okay time— and you'll be delighted by what you start learning about yourself.

TRUST YOUR INSTINCTS

We've suggested this before, but it's so vital it's worth bringing up again. Instinct—the little voice that always steers a person in the right direction—is your most important ally. It is not critical, nor judgmental, nor even rational. It simply knows, on a subconscious level, what's best for you, and tells you. You can never put one over on instinct, because it is the truest reflection of who you are. It's something everyone is born with, and is set up to help human beings survive. All you have to do is learn to listen to it.

Say your husband calls every afternoon at about five, just to chat. You don't want to cut off contact, but having to go through the charade of pretending everything's fine when it isn't (after all, he's living with another woman) is driving you crazy. Then, too, you may even have a gut feeling it isn't doing your goal—getting him back—any good. *Respect* that instinct. You don't need to be hostile; just explain, sweetly, that you care too much to play games. You're okay, you hope he's okay, but it's too painful for you to act as if nothing has happened, so would he please not call unless he really has something to say. This shows him you care, but also that you have a life of your own going, and aren't as needy as he seems to think—which should both confuse and intrigue him. He'll keep calling, all right—but not "just to chat."

The same applies to meeting new people. If you have the instant sense that somebody's a bore, or a neurotic, why waste time? Better to stay home with a juicy novel.

WRITE AWAY THE BLUES

Another great ally in tough times is a diary. A new study at Southern Methodist University in Dallas shows that writing down painful experiences as they occur, as well as the feelings—guilt, jealousy—that accompany them, helps dissipate such emotions. James W. Pennebaker, the psychologist who conducted the study, found that students who participated felt that writing helped them organize and clarify their thoughts, as well as confront what was troubling them.

Pennebaker also found that writing about traumas improves physical health. He did a follow-up study that showed that the immune system T-cells that fight bacteria and viruses became more efficient as the students worked out their conflicts by writing about them. So keeping a diary can help you feel better in more ways than one.

Don't worry if you miss writing for a day or two—no one's giving you a grade. It's overall consistency that counts. Just try to jot down what happened, and how it made you feel, on a regular basis. Improvement is often unbelievably quick—when you look back over what you wrote only a few weeks ago, you may be surprised at how much better you already feel. Spelling, sentence structure, and punctuation don't matter here, so don't even think about them. You're not writing for posterity. You're writing for *you*.

One final point. We've noticed that no matter how smart or talented a woman may be, those who really succeed are the ones who follow up. You know how impressive it is when you run into a friend who says "Oh, I'll send you that article on foot reflexology," and she does, right? Or what about the co-worker who offers to help you out when you're swamped—and that neatly typed report is on your desk the next morning. These people move ahead, not just in work or social situations but in all life areas. They also feel good about themselves, and see themselves as competent, worthwhile human beings.

So it's not going to do you any good to say "Sure, I'll talk to more new people, or find a therapist, or keep a diary, or buy a puppy, but not right away." You have to get going now. Procrastination can be like an invasive disease—it gets worse if you don't do anything about it. Fight it! Make up your mind to do whatever it is you've said you'll do, and then *do it*. Pretty soon, followup will become a habit—one that leaves you feeling smugly proud about how efficient and effective you are.

CHAPTER 6

The Plan:

A Nine-Step,

Surefire

Formula for

Getting Him

Back

Now comes the time to put your newfound sense of power into operation. But before we get into specifics, it's important to note that however much stronger you feel, however shored up your belief in your own value as a person, you are probably going to feel shakier at this point than at any other. Why? Because everything you're striving for is on the line. In a very real sense, this is it—you are now actively going to follow a plan designed to win him back, and fears of being rejected, of making a fool of yourself, may become so overwhelming at times that it may seem easier—and safer—to retreat to a course of nonaction. That way, you put off facing the possibility, slim though it may be, that the relationship really is over. Better to delay, to dream about the day you and he will be back together, you reason, than to take reality into your own hands and go for broke.

The problem is, fantasizing about a husband or lover returning on his own, without any input on your part, although superficially comforting, leaves you in limbo. Say he does eventually come home. Because you've done nothing to effect this change of heart, you won't know *why* he's back. Nor will you be convinced it will last. You'll never be sure if he's sincere, or if his girlfriend threw him out, or what. Obviously, such passive acceptance is an extremely fragile basis upon which to build a new and better relationship.

Then, too, you may waste precious months, even years, locked in a self-destructive waiting game, putting your life on hold as you look forward to the day he'll walk in the door bearing roses, drop to his knees, and beg your forgiveness—just like in the movies! Real life, however, rarely approaches the movies. And while fantasizing certainly has its uses, it's highly suspect in this case because it prevents you from living.

Also, taking on such a passive role is bound to make you feel rotten—as if you're just a feather in the wind, helplessly buffeted about by fate. Far better, we feel, to *act,* even if that posture does entail some risks.

If you've assessed your own feelings about wanting your man back, and thought hard about why he strayed, those risks are minimal. You already know you and he could have a future together. To ensure that you do have one, you must confront your fears—just as you previously found the courage to confront your man about the affair—and move forward. For the relationship is not all that will die if you don't; your sense of self-worth is at stake.

"In any situation you have a choice between (1) being effective and reaching your goals, or (2) being ineffective and, ultimately, being restricted from doing what you desire," says Wayne Dyer. "In most cases—not all, but most—you can be effective and in *all* cases, you can operate *from the position of your own intrinsic worth as a person*" (italics ours).

Dyer goes on to say that every time you reach inward and come up with a "fear sentence," that is, "I'll fail . . ." "I'll look stupid . . ." "I'll lose everything . . ." "I might get hurt", it means you've consulted your "weakness mentality," and that old victim stamp is once again on you.

"If you have to have a guarantee that everything will be all right before you take a risk," notes Dyer, "you will never get to first base, because the future is promised to no one. There are no guarantees on life's services to you, so you'll have to toss away your panicky thoughts if you want to get what you want out of life. Moreover, almost all your fearful thoughts are purely head trips. The disasters you envision will rarely surface. Remember the ancient sage who said, "I'm an old man, and I've had many troubles, most of which have never happened.' "

You're having troubles right now, of course—lots of them. They *are* happening, and we don't mean to minimize that fact. But in a larger sense, Dyer's point is well taken. Because you've put a great deal of time and thought into figuring out what went wrong in your relationship, you've learned that old fears about being rejected, "losing," are almost certain to be groundless. To get what you want, you *cannot* let panic prevent you from acting.

To minimize such panic, Dyer and other experts suggest you ask yourself: "What is the worst thing that could happen to me if. . . ." In your case, the worst thing that could happen would be to wind up without your man. But—to put it bluntly—you don't have him now, anyway, right? So if you fail in your quest, you'll just be back where you started, in a situation you're already dealing with, and probably handling quite well. Given this fact, why not get out there and try?

"You will never know what it feels like to get rid of a fear until you risk behavior that confronts it," says Dyer. "You can talk to your therapist until you turn into a frog, you can brood until your teeth itch, and your brain sweats . . . but you'll never understand until you *do*."

You don't, by the way, have to feel all that courageous, especially at the start. Just get going. *Behave* as if you were fearless, and, as in other areas (confidence, friendliness), the quality will eventually filter down from the outside in. In other words, act as if you were brave, and you'll soon *be* brave. (Nobody knows exactly why this trick works, but it does.)

Remember, too, that you're approaching our nine-step formula with a lot of ammunition—new insights about yourself, your man, the relationship, newly discovered strengths. It isn't as if you're jumping off a diving board without knowing how to swim—you're going in *prepared*.

Finally, keep repeating those vital percentages we mentioned earlier: 75 to 85 percent of men don't leave permanently; 80 percent long to remarry the woman they left. This will see you through many a bad moment. By beginning our plan—right now—you are maximizing the chances that *your* man will be among the majority of those who come back. You're ready to get out there and give it all you've got—honestly, you are. So go ahead. Just do it. Here's how:

NINE SUREFIRE WAYS TO WIN HIM BACK

1. STAY COOL: REMEMBER THAT YOU HAVE MUCH MORE POWER THAN YOU THINK

Again, nothing, but nothing, is as attractive to a confused, errant husband or lover than a cool, in-control woman. He'll be taken off-guard—how can you behave this way, when he'd expected tears, pleas, recriminations, the sort of tactics that probably would have sent him sprinting into the other woman's arms. Your composure alone is instantly intriguing, and intriguing is definitely what you want to be. By refusing to come across as desperate, you give your man enough distance to be able to take a fresh look at you—to remember what he loved about you in the first place. It is most important that you give him the chance to see you as a strong, separate, desirable woman. If you appear in such a light, your every contact with him will be so pleasant and memorable, he'll want to return for more.

Certainly, there will be times you'll fall apart, but try very, very hard not to lose control in front of your man. *Desire, not pity, is what you want him to feel;* coming across as pathetic and needy never got a woman much of anywhere. Oh, it's true that some men may be lured back by the "Help! I-can't-make-it-alone" plea (whether out of genuine compassion or their own need to feel powerful), but pity soon turns to a sense of being trapped, and often, to downright disgust. (We know it isn't pleasant to hear such truths, but better now than later. And getting your man back aside, "helpless" is *not* the sort of woman you want to be.) So have hysterics at the shrink's; tell a close friend how panicky you are; weep during group therapy sessions; call him every name in the book in the privacy of your kitchen, and hurl a few pots for added emphasis. But make a big effort not to lose it when your man is around. If, during a particularly painful moment, you do let him see your fear or rage, forgive yourself, and the next time around, show him your new, cooler image. It's the same as going off a diet—a pint of chocolate chocolate chip ice cream is not going to kill you as long as you're back to grapefruit and protein toast the following morning.

"I don't think he had the slightest idea how petrified I was," says one woman we talked to, who, for obvious reasons, didn't want her name used—her husband *still* doesn't know:

> One time, before I was supposed to meet him for a drink to talk about the kids, I went on a total crying jag. When it was finally over, my face was all blotchy and swollen to about twice its normal size; my eyes were slits. But then I filled the washbasin with ice cubes and water, and kept splashing and splashing my face. Then lying down, with tea bags on my eyes, I tried to pull myself together. Finally, I did the makeup number of my life. And all the while, I kept saying to myself, "I will not give him the satisfaction of seeing me in this shape; I *will* not; I *will* not." Well, thank God for Lancôme and Elizabeth Arden. When I breezed—breezed, hah!; my heart was beating so fast, it was practically fibrillating—into the bar, he was already there, and I saw this sort of surprised look on his face, as if he were thinking, "What's with her? Here she is all fixed

up and standing tall and smiling. . . . Isn't she supposed to be pale and teary and desperate?" I got quite a kick out of that.

Psyching yourself by repeating a positive phrase over and over, as this woman did ("I will not give him the satisfaction" or "I am strong" or "Smile. There's no time for tears") is often helpful before any contact with your man. So is visualization. Whenever you know you'll be meeting him, start picturing yourself in a cool mode—actually *see* yourself dealing with the situation calmly, confidently, as if you were watching yourself on a movie screen. If you can also picture the physical setting you'll be in, so much the better. Some visualization experts say "color pictures" work better than black and white; most feel that just before bed is a prime time to hold such pictures in your mind, although if it's possible to set aside quiet moments during the day when you can really concentrate hard, that's fine, too.

Practicing what you're going to say, and how you're going to say it, is helpful as well. Think of all the topics your man is likely to bring up, and then rehearse your reactions in front of a mirror. You might even write a little script, and have a trusted friend read "his" parts so that you can respond aloud.

Choose your meeting times with care. You want to avoid facing your man if you're stressed out because your day began with root canal and segued into driving six hyper little boys to soccer practice. Many women find it soothing to schedule a therapy session just before contact.

You'd have to be a saint not to react when the man you love and want back is rambling on like an idiot about how he's "found himself," or intimating how happy he is, so *you* direct the conversation. That way, if he initiates any details about what he's up to, you can stop him in mid-sentence. Don't allow him to verbalize his feelings about the other woman, because it helps him make the situation real—which is exactly what you don't want. And for heaven's sake, don't you ask questions about her or his new life, either, no matter how much you're dying to know—the answers are certain to have you hurling china.

Finally, be aware that many extremely sane, sensible women have gone pretty crazy over a spouse's affair. One wife, when she saw her husband's girlfriend sporting a pair of gorgeous, diamond-studded earrings, reached out in a rage and ripped them off the woman's ears. The torn lobes required stitches, and the wife wound up in court. Another wife made menacing late-night phone calls to her "replacement"; still another found out the girlfriend's address, and sent her a package containing a voodoo doll stuck with pins. Aside from being distasteful—and in some cases, dangerous—that sort of revenge invariably backfires.

"The irony," psychologist Paul Hauck pointed out, in a June 27, 1991, article in the *Daily News,* "is that the mate is repelled by the ex's jealousy and possessiveness, qualities that may have driven him off in the first place." Another irony, added New York City divorce lawyer Bernard Clair in the same piece, "is that an ex's harassment often tends to make the current couple closer, as they commiserate on an ex's wacky behavior."

So do your best not to turn your man off, or give him and the girlfriend anything to commiserate about. However much you'd like to follow the script in *Presumed Innocent* (in which the wife kills her husband's lover in an effort to recapture his love), remember that "wacky"—or worse—is definitely not the image you're after.

2. BUY TIME

More good news: time is on your side. You know the odds are with you, so be patient and avoid boxing your man into a corner with such ultimatums as, "If you don't leave that slut this minute, we're through." The more time you give your husband or lover (all the while working hard, of course, to change the situation), the more time he has to see that you are the one he really wants, and the more time the other woman has to hang herself. Often, after just a few months, one of the two will simply get sick to death of the other—more often him than her.

"For the majority of other women, the waiting seems to hurt

more than it helps," says Marion Zola. *Keep her waiting as long as possible.* Tell your man that with so much at stake, the very least he can do is give your relationship another year, six months, even three months if that's all he'll agree to. Perspectives shift dramatically with time—what may seem like insurmountable differences today often shrink to nothing with a little distance, and it's up to you to make sure that distance happens. Remember that you are the more rational partner at this point. He may be picturing sunsets and moonglow and love everlasting, but you know it can't last. You could therefore say you almost have a duty to save him from himself.

"Without question, I had to force myself to be a grownup," says Caroline, who waited out her husband's affair for eight months—and won. "Yes, it took a lot of strength; yes, it was hard to demand time when my wounded pride was telling me to throw all his clothes out the window onto the front lawn and yell, 'Get out of my life forever!' But however idiotically he was behaving, I knew our marriage was worth hanging onto. And it worked."

Adds Maggie, "I told him, 'Look, you may not believe this now, but I know what you're going through, and I promise you, Jonathan, I'll literally make you a bet, I'll give you five hundred dollars if I'm wrong—you won't feel this way in six months. Naturally, I wasn't wrong, and now we're back together. A little bruised, maybe, but together."

If your man is hell-bent on a legal separation or divorce, you can slow him down in more concrete ways, as well. Cancel meetings. Put off signing papers. Have your lawyer take his or her time questioning fine points. One woman we talked with told us that when the separation papers were finally ready to be signed, the other woman was long gone, and her husband was already making coming-home noises.

The bit point to remember, as we've so often said, is that such affairs almost never last. In a March 1991 *Cosmopolitan* article called "A Married Man's Advice to Single Girls: Beware!," writer Ben Stein told of a friend Lenny, who lives down the street from him in Santa Monica. Lenny sells deals, but his real job, ever since he got married, has been to be a married man who has single girlfriends. He says it's about ten times easier for a married man to seduce women than for a single man: "Having a wife . . . validates me to them. I'm not just a single loser nerd. She tells them I'm worth having."

But Lenny goes on to explain that while he really loves the girls with whom he has affairs, it never works.

> Maybe it's about just being used to my wife. Maybe it's because when you start out a relationship with the girlfriend in the back alley, she's eventually going to get resentful and jealous. That's a lot of it. They all start out saying they know the score, that they don't expect anything, but they all, always, every single time, expect you're going to leave your wife and marry them. When you don't they get furious. They get angry. They start spying on you. They attempt suicide. They threaten my wife. They even threaten my daughter.
>
> Every single part of the dynamic that made them so appealing gets turned upside down. They're not an escape hatch any longer. They're the Gestapo, checking your every move, ten times as suspicious as your wife, because after all, they *know* you cheat. And all that anger they buried at first comes roaring out. Instead of that freeing feeling, you get an impending doom feeling.

We hope your husband or lover doesn't go from girlfriend to girlfriend, as Lenny does. Even he says "it's like an addiction," and that he wishes he could learn to get over it. But otherwise, Lenny's story of what happens in such affairs is classic: everything that made the other woman seem so appealing at the start—her ease, sense of fun, value as an escape hatch—soon degenerates into threats, resentment, fury. And when the man has had enough, which usually doesn't take long, it's over. Buy yourself the time it takes for your man to say, "It's over." Doing that isn't in the least degrading (you're demanding, remember, not begging); you have some very real rights here.

3. START GROWING

Initially, it might seem strange to look upon this painful period as an opportunity for exceptional personal growth—a time to effect large-scale positive changes in your life—but that's what every expert we spoke with strongly advises. In a very real sense, your man's return, although it may be your overt aim, should be considered a by-product; you are using this period for *yourself.* And by so doing, you invariably wind up with the man as well. In case after case of the women interviewed, this proved to be true. Listen to Marcie, a thirty-four-year-old assistant art director:

> The first few months were awful. Awful. But then I started thinking, not so much about David, as myself. I'd never really been alone in my whole life before; maybe it was my first chance to do some assessing. I had a job, but not work I truly cared about. I had acquaintances, but no close friends. I'd been Marcie the wife, who was a terrific cook and never refused to make love; Marcie the super-Mom; Marcie the executive assistant who cheerfully took on every bit of extra work the office had to offer, but I'd never been *there*— not anywhere. And that had to have been part of what was wrong with our marriage.
>
> I think what happened to me during the seven months David was gone is what made him want to come back. Slowly, slowly, I started to change. I began to stand up for myself at work, and what do you know, the world didn't collapse. I asked my mother to babysit two nights a week— something I'd never allowed myself to ask of her before— and took a course in layout and design, which I'd always been interested in. I started to make new friends, real ones, the sort of friends I could confide in, tell what was wrong as well as what was right about my life. I even began to look different—smiled more, stood straighter, took more interest in my clothes.
>
> If all of this sounds like magic, it wasn't. There were

times I was so miserable I thought I couldn't live another day without David. But every day I did live without him gave me courage. In three words, what happened was that I grew up. And I finally knew that no matter what, whether David came back or not, I'd be okay.

Then one night, when David had taken the kids to a movie, I was late getting home from class, and they were there, all three of them, waiting for me when I burst in— really happy because the instructor had complimented me in front of everybody on a design I'd done. And I must have looked kind of glowing and excited, because they all stared at me, and then David said, in that special way he has, "Well, look who's home." And from that moment on, I knew it was over with the girl he'd been seeing. I knew it would eventually work out.

When Marcie realized that she could live without David (not wanted to, just could), she took a giant step toward growth. For although the more obvious ways to start growing—reinvestigating talents and interests that have been put on hold; reaching out to others—are vital, having the courage to be alone is the very essence of growth. Once you understand that no one, not even a husband or lover, can or will "be there" for you at all times, in every way; once you see that your main relationship is and always will be with yourself, fears and panic recede. Only then is it possible to use alone-time productively, and you'll even actively seek it out.

Whether in or out of a relationship, every woman needs such quiet moments to find out who she is and where she's going. Setting aside special time is the only way to get to know yourself, get in touch with your true feelings, learn to love yourself, if you will.

"Without time alone, we become confused as to who we are," says Carolyn Bushong. "We feel empty because we don't have an intimate relationship with ourselves. Then we feel scattered and unclear when dealing with others because we have no solid core; therefore, when we're around others constantly, we become reflections of them. We end up so confused that we don't know who we are or what we want from someone else. Reflecting our identities off of others can also be incredibly draining. Once you take the time alone to know yourself, you will find that your time alone will give you energy and help you stay strong and 'on track' in your relationships."

Bushong adds that aloneness is a requirement for facing fears and issues, and working through them. "Only when we're alone can we get in touch with our feelings of insecurity so that we can overcome them. Only when we're in touch with these insecurities can we become clear about a direct course of action needed to take charge of our lives."

This doesn't mean you should isolate yourself from others—far from it. Nor does it mean you should wallow in insecurities and fears. What it does mean is that by setting aside specific times each day to be alone (that way, *you're* controlling when and how), you'll be better able to deal with whatever life hands out. Whether you opt for twenty minutes or an hour will vary—some people need to be alone more than others—but just as with exercise, the key word is *regular*.

4. KEEP IN CLOSE CONTACT

We've advised that you give your man some emotional distance, but at the same time you have to militantly maintain contact. Out of sight can be out of mind, and if, through passivity or to minimize anguish, you avoid your husband or lover, or allow him to avoid you, you make it that much easier for him to sever ties.

There are many ways, both sneaky and otherwise, to stay in close touch. You need to discuss the children (he's their father, after all), the household insurance (who else can you trust?), how to reframe that Hockney print (he has such great taste). Just because he's temporarily behaving like a rebellious two-year-old doesn't mean you have to switch health clubs, either (just be sure to *be* there whenever he's signed up for racquetball). If he's already moved out, you send cards, clippings, notes. You invite him for

Thanksgiving dinner . . . for the kids' sake. You make certain he's included in parent conferences, invited to school plays, Father's Day, athletic events. On his birthday, you hand-deliver the Sony shower radio he's always wanted. You suggest meeting him for a quick lunch "just to catch up," and make a reservation at the charming little French place where you had so many fun lunches in the past. By staying in constant contact—*and making each contact enjoyable*—you eliminate the possibility that he will remember only the God-awful moments of your relationship (which, if you've gotten to this point, you have to admit must have been more than a few) and compare them to the heady new "single" life he currently thinks he's having.

Will it be easy to make each contact enjoyable? No! You will often have to mentally grit your teeth and smile seductively when you'd rather be yelling. You will often fall apart when you get home. But remember, you are making all this effort for a greater good—getting your man back where he belongs. Also, many women told us that, oddly enough, they became so adept at playing this fun, sexy, charm-girl role, their encounters with husbands and lovers actually *became* pleasant—for themselves as well as for their men. "I think somehow the actress in me took over," Kathy a thirty-eight-year-old lab technician from St. Paul, Minnesota, told us:

> Suddenly, I wasn't the tired, grumpy, over-worked mom I'd often been when Andrew got home from work. Whenever we'd get together to talk about the kids or the broken lawn mower, or whatever, I'd make a point of being relaxed, warm, even flirtatious—more the way I'd been when we were first going out together. This was really tough at first because the fact that he'd been "intimate" with another woman was just about driving me crazy, but I simply forced myself to stop thinking about that and to try to concentrate on the things about Andrew I'd always loved, like his dimples, his wonderful, warm laughter, and his quick, analytical mind. The more I concentrated on the good stuff, the more

he felt it—at least on some intuitive level—and we started to have a little fun on some of our get-togethers.

The funny thing was that after a while, I didn't feel so much like an actress anymore. I realized I'd been pretty hard on Andrew sometimes, and that it was healthy to get dressed up for, and be playful with, your own husband. Somewhere, deep down inside, I knew that I had to keep it light. This was no time for recriminations—honey, not vinegar, was the order of the day. And, it really worked. Andrew began to call more often, and seemed more relaxed than he'd been in years. I think that underneath it all, we started to get back in touch with what had attracted us to each other in the first place. It was a great feeling, and we both knew it.

If your man turns you down the first time you suggest meeting, or doesn't react to a note or phone call, just keep at it. (Although it's a good idea to space your feelers out, so that he doesn't feel *bombarded*—one a week or every ten days is probably enough.) Nobody likes to be rejected, especially by someone one loves, but eventually, he's bound to come around.

We hope it goes without saying that the other woman is never included in any of these contacts. You are not about to give her the chance to start having a relationship with your children— or with you. (You'd be amazed at how often a girlfriend will try to ingratiate herself; even more stunned at how often a man who's strayed will try to make her "part of the family.")

5. LET HIM KNOW YOU LOVE AND NEED HIM

This is often difficult, especially when you're feeling so hurt and vulnerable, but you have to remember that it's the *long-term love bond* between you two, bruised though it may be, that will finally win him back. You can be sure "the other woman" is telling him how much she loves and needs him, so be fierce in pointing out that your love is deeper, stronger, based not on infatuation but on feelings that grew during a valid, sickness-and-health relationship. No one will ever love him the way you do. No one! This is one of the key cards you have to play. You know him in a way she cannot. You need him in a way she cannot. Don't forget that needing him isn't the same as *being* needy—certainly, you want to continue to come across as a vibrant, independent woman. But it's possible that the fact he *was* needed—and loved—got lost in the scramble of day-to-day living. Not just needed to pay half the rent or start the car on subzero mornings, but needed as a lover, friend, person. So you make it clear that you can live without him, but would definitely rather not. You must make him feel valued again—by word, gesture, and any ammunition you've got—not for services rendered, but for *himself*.

"I honestly don't think he realized I cared all that much," says Terrie, a forty-one-year-old investment banker:

> When he told me he'd fallen in love with someone else, a woman he worked with, and wanted a divorce, my first instinct was just to cave in. But then, somehow, I heard myself saying that I loved him too much ever to let him go without a fight. That was obviously the last response he'd expected—you've never seen a man look so stunned. It was actually kind of heartbreaking. I guess he thought it would all be easy—I'd agree to a divorce without any fuss because, after all, I didn't really care one way or the other, and he'd go on to play happy families with a new woman who'd be the kids' second Mommy. I made very, very sure he saw that wouldn't be the case.

We heard many stories like Terrie's—cases in which the man had not been aware of how much his wife or lover cared. (Many women, of course, aren't aware of how much their men care either, but that's not what we're concerned with here). One reason for this growing phenomenon is that contemporary women are particularly vulnerable when it comes to falling into the "don't show it" trap. These days, the whole concept of love has got more than a little mixed up. To fully express love is thought to be rather naïve, a sign of weakness. Coupled with this notion is the feeling that giving (which, in essence, is what love is) somehow entails giving up. Having made such huge advances over the past two decades in terms of independence, many women are wary of showing they care because they see love as a sacrifice, along the same lines of doing all the housework or putting a man's needs before their own—the sort of stereotypical role-playing they've fought so long and hard against.

But giving—by which we mean loving—is far from a sign of weakness. Instead, it is, as Erich Fromm writes in *The Art of Loving,* the highest expression of potency.

> In the very act of giving. I experience my strength, my wealth, my power. This experience of heightened vitality and potency fills me with joy. I experience myself as overflowing, spending, alive, hence as joyous. Giving is more joyous than receiving, not because it is a deprivation, but because in the act of giving lies the expression of my aliveness.
>
> What does one person give to another? He gives of himself, of the most precious he has, he gives of his life. This does not necessarily mean that he sacrifices his life for the other—but that he gives him of that which is alive in him; he gives him of his joy, of his interest, of his understanding, of his knowledge, of his humor, of his sadness— of all expressions and manifestations of that which is alive in him. In thus giving of his life, he enriches the other person, he enhances the other's sense of aliveness by enhancing his own sense of aliveness. . . . Specifically with regard to love this means: *love is a power which produces love* (italics ours).

Fromm goes on to say that mature love, by definition, is a relationship in which each partner's integrity and individuality are preserved, and explains the difference between infantile and mature love: "Infantile love follows the principle: '*I love because*

I am loved.' Mature love follows the principle: *'I am loved because I love.'* Immature love says: *'I love you because I need you.'* Mature love says: *'I need you because I love you.'* "

This beautiful book, first published in 1956, is more valid today than ever, and we recommend that you go out and find a copy. Along with his theories on love, Fromm takes the reader through each step of how to put those theories into practice—you actually "learn" how to love, the same way you'd learn any other art. Don't be put off by the slightly "biblical" tone—the man knows what he's talking about.

It's scary to start showing love when you've been hurt, and aren't sure of the reaction you'll get, but now's the time to summon up all your strength, stop worrying about being "un-liberated," and dive in. Don't be afraid to love, and to let him know it—not just because you want him back, but for your *own* joy.

6. MAKE HIM A LITTLE JEALOUS

Throughout this nine-step program, the image you want to project is not that of a downtrodden mate who's always available, but of a lively, confident, sexy woman whom *he* might not get back if he isn't careful. Can you do this while still showing him how much you love and need him? Of course! Whoever said you had to be a one-note woman? Keeping your man a bit off-balance, even if he's the only one you truly want, is just another ploy in the great game of getting him back—like staying cool (when you don't feel cool at all) or making contacts enjoyable (when at times you're ready to toss your glass of beaujolais nouveau in his face). But the bonus in this case is that it can be *fun* and will do wonders for your self-esteem. We don't mean you should arrange to have him walk in on you and another man in bed, or talk endlessly about the fabulous new lover you've supposedly found (that's playing with fire), just that creating a little jealousy in your man definitely doesn't hurt. It's simply human nature to find desirable what someone else finds desirable, whether it's a person, a neighborhood, even this year's trendy breed of dog. So unless you're out to disprove basic sociobiology, don't sit around worrying about *why* and *if,* and get on with it.

Reverse the situation for a minute and think of the time you saw your man deep in conversation with that attractive woman at the cocktail party. Only an hour before, you'd been looking him over as he got dressed and thinking, "God, Ken's really letting himself go lately. He must have put on ten pounds, and it's all in his middle. I wonder if he's going to wear the same old blah gray suit. Oh, well. Nobody will notice. He always hugs the wall at parties and never talks to anybody, anyway." But one glance at him chatting with a pretty woman who seemed charmed by him, and he took on a whole new glow, didn't he? Well, so will *you* if your man sees that another man's interested.

If there's any way for you to dance, talk, or laugh with a cute man in your husband or lover's presence, do so. Maybe nobody knows about his affair, and you still go out together for "appearance's sake." Then get yourself on the dance floor at the country club, work the room at a party, give your dinner partner your undivided attention as if he were the only male on earth. (Touching his arm lightly to make a point, brushing his hand with yours, wins you even more points). The idea is to surprise your man, show him you're desirable—and that you won't always be there, waiting, proverbial slippers in one hand and perfectly mixed martini in the other.

"Don't be afraid to create a little suspense and intrigue. Don't hang on his every whim or try to please him all the time. This gets boring to men. Don't be available all the time. Let him wonder about your love and desire for him occasionally," advise California psychologists Connell Cowan and Melvyn Kinder in *Women Men Love . . . Women Men Leave.* "This won't endanger your relationship, it will cause him to be more respectful, attentive and interested. . . . Remember, by creating reminders of your separate identity and desires, you will maintain the psychological space that will motivate him to move toward you."

Why do you think it was that in the past, your man often seemed to get turned on at the weirdest times—while you were talking on the phone with a girlfriend, for instance, or engrossed in a made-for-TV movie, or trying to take a bubble bath in peace? *Because you weren't paying attention to him.* Take the concept one step further—pay attention to someone else instead of him—and you're sure to get him going.

More tips: You're meeting him for drinks to discuss summer camps for Susie? (And you will make sure that you do meet for drinks to discuss summer camps for Susie, even if Susie has already chosen her own camp, thank you very much.) You arrive breathless, a little late, looking terrific. When he asks why you're late—which he very probably will—you seem flustered. You let mention of a fun weekend in the country slip out, then seem *doubly* flustered. You arrange to have a girlfriend call when you know he'll be at your place, have a quick, *sotto voce* conversation, then return to the room, eyes averted. You hear his voice on your answering machine late at night, and don't pick up. If he calls in the morning, you *do* pick up, answering sensuously, sleepily, putting your hand half over the receiver and whispering a one-liner (not too blatantly graphic, though), to the fantasy lover lying next to you. Isn't all this, well, just a little dishonest? Definitely. But it isn't exactly honest for a man to cheat on his wife or girlfriend, either. Nor is it honest of the other woman to try to steal your man. You owe the girlfriend nothing and don't ever forget it, so anything that will get your man back is fair game. Just don't get silly or overdo it.

7. DON'T ADD TO THE PRESSURE HE'S ALREADY UNDER

No, he's not free, nor are you about to let him become so, but you have to make a superhuman effort to avoid issuing the ultimate ultimatum: It's either her or me . . . and the kids, the house, the Toyota. We've touched on this previously, and also talked about the Pressure Cooker Crunch in chapter 3 (which you might want to refer to again, because even if that isn't why your man left, much of the advice still applies). But it's a particularly vital point to remember right now because you're actively engaged in trying to win him back, and want a resolution of this wrenching situation *fast*. Such pressure, however, will only make him want to run even more. Although it's true that ultimatums have sometimes pushed men into returning, it's usually because they were ready to come back in the first place. (If not, even if they do come back, they're not likely to stay.) Trying to scare him by suggesting a trial separation (assuming he hasn't actually left) isn't a good idea, either—if he's still at home, you want to try to keep him there. But wherever he is—at home, in his own apartment, in *her* apartment—the main thing is: *Keep the heat off*.

Suzie, a fifty-two-year-old photographer from Connecticut, remembers:

> I don't think I'd ever felt so disoriented in my whole life. John was living with some woman from his office and all our friends knew about it. At first I was humiliated, then furious, and sometimes, when we'd be talking on the phone, I'd get an overwhelming urge to become hysterical. "I'm not putting up with this for one more second!" I wanted to yell. I kept fighting it though, since this marvelous shrink I'd found kept reminding me that panic, pressuring him, would never bring him back. So I just acted cool, even though I felt like threatening to firebomb his office.
>
> Then one Saturday, about two months after he'd left, we were having lunch at a pub to talk about our youngest daughter's college applications, and something felt different. He wasn't so shifty-eyed anymore, didn't seem as anxious. And he was really listening to what I had to say. I had the feeling the balance of power had switched, that maybe things weren't going so smoothly with the teenybopper (which was how I liked to think of her) and I almost suggested that maybe it was time for him to come back home. But I didn't. Some little voice told me not to push— to leave well enough alone and give him enough room to come to his own conclusions. This newfound self-control

amazed even me, but I knew it was the best way to handle the situation—and I was right. Three weeks later, John called late one evening and said he had to talk to me; could he come right over? Again, the picture of self-control. I said I thought his coming over so late might upset the kids, but I'd be happy to meet him for breakfast the next morning at the McDonald's in our neighborhood. When we met, he announced that he'd made a terrible mistake, that he really loved me, and the kids, and the life we'd had together more than anything and if I would only give him a second chance, he wanted to come back and pick up where we left off.

I was so happy I could hardly contain myself and told him so, but I also told him that there were a lot of things we'd have to talk about and work out before he could actually move back in. That was two years ago, and I know it sounds sappy, but we have a great relationship now and I'm secretly very proud of myself for not falling apart, and for being such a laidback but loving lady.

Other types of pressure, such as demands for attention (*"Please* come over; I'm so lonely I could die"); services ("The washing machine is flooded and I don't know what to do"); acts of violence (spraypainting the girlfriend's front door; cutting the crotches out of his pants and mailing them to her—as one woman ruefully admitted she did) not only don't work, they're demeaning, don't make you feel good about yourself.

Some women told us they'd pressured their men to have sex, and in retrospect, fervently wish they hadn't. "I had it all planned," says Ashley. "I called and told him I needed to see him right away—on what pretext, I can't remember. Anyway, when he rang the bell, there I was, waiting, in my shortest miniskirt, and no underwear. He was hardly in the door before I had my arms around him, and I was going, 'please, sleep with me; please, just once; just this one last time.' God, it was degrading. I can't believe I did it. Well, we did wind up having sex, but as soon as it was over, he got dressed, not looking at me, and said he had to go. I lay in bed for hours, crying. . . ."

As we all know, sex is a potent hold, but trying to manipulate your man into making love is almost always a bad idea, so fight the impulse. The less you pressure him in *any* way, the better off you'll be. One bright note is that the other woman is probably pressuring him hourly, so—irony or ironies—he may begin to see his relationship with *you* as the true path to freedom.

8. BE HIS BEST FRIEND

Since you've been his best friend for a long time—or were until recently—this shouldn't be too difficult. You have to show your man you understand how hard all this is for him, too. It's not that you want him to think you *like* what he's doing; rather, you realize that telling him he's the biggest son-of-a-bitch on earth will not bring him home. Think of the way you handle a friend, or a child, who's behaving badly. Somehow, you're able to show you love and support the person, while at the same time making it clear you don't condone his or her actions. The same theory applies here. If your man says the other woman is pressuring him, using all the childish tactics you've so wisely avoided— tears, tantrums, threats—you serenely commiserate, then get off the subject as quickly as possible and into something more fun, more sexy, than the tasteless ploys of a desperate woman. (You never bring her up, by the way, and permit him to do so as little as possible—preferably never. She is not a part of his real life.) You're supportive when he brings up worries about children, money, what friends will say—supportive, but not acquiescent because, after all, these worries are valid, and you want him to remember that fact. The last thing you're after is to make all this easy for him. What you do want is to be an island of calm and pleasure in his increasingly tortured life. Isn't that what friends are for?

"The hardest part for me," says Theresa, a fifty-nine-year-old history teacher from Denver, "was that Todd never actually moved out."

I knew about the other woman—we'd talked about her, briefly, a couple of times—but it had never gotten to the point where he said he wanted to leave. This meant we were together a lot—at dinner most nights, weekends at our cabin in the mountains—so there were times when I found keeping my cool almost impossible.

I did have a couple of close friends in whom I confided, and that really saved my life. One of them, bless her, kept reminding me of what good friends Todd and I'd always seemed to be. She was right about that. Until very recently, we'd shared everything in our thirty-year marriage, so I made a deal with myself to keep up the friendship part no matter what else was happening. I drew the line, though, when it came to talking about "her." I wanted it to be perfectly clear that I was not his accomplice in this nasty business. Hard as it was, I think he respected me for that. Even when the affair was over, I didn't want to know much about it. I figured, "why do that to myself?" There had already been quite enough pain, thank you, and the last thing I wanted to do was wallow in it. I think Todd wanted to talk it all out so I could forgive him, but I just couldn't handle it, and he figured that out pretty quickly. Now, it's been three years, and it's almost as if what he did never happened. Some shrinks would probably tell me that wasn't a healthy way to deal with the whole thing, but for me, there just didn't seem to be much choice.

9. REMIND HIM OF THE GOOD TIMES

Include the sexy ones. That unbelievable night in Maui after skinny-dipping. You shake your head. Will it ever be that way for either of you again? (Thereby implying that you, too, have other options.) The wild, secret stuff you used to do in the laundry room together. The time he told you about his Sir Gawain fantasy, and what happened after *that*. (Don't, however, actually sleep with him, no matter how turned on he gets. If you just casually fall into bed with him at this stage, you lose a major drawing card.) Reminders don't have to be verbal, either—smells, tastes, sights, sounds, settings will all jar a man's memory. Does the evening you sipped champagne and ate roast duck in front of a crackling fire stand out? Slip a duck into the oven; light a fire in the fireplace! Do Bob Marley tapes bring back memories of a fabulous Caribbean holiday? Play the tapes! Does the sight of fall leaves have special meaning? Invite him for a walk on a crisp October day! Wear the perfume you wore when you were dating, the bracelet he gave you on your anniversary, over drinks in a sun-splashed café.

Remind him of the other good times, too—those warm, loving moments that stand out in every couple's relationship. They may have to do with a weekend alone together, a child, a triumph shared. As Diane Vaughan points out, "No relationship is all bad. Moments always exist when the two partners are brought together in an experience that is sometimes surprising in its meaningfulness. At such times, both partners recognize the importance of the bond and the shared history that led to that moment." Even more important, Vaughan notes that for initiators of a breakup, such experiences inject contradictory information into the negative definitions he's been constructing. "As a consequence," says Vaughan, "they are forced to acknowledge the positive aspects of life with the other person. Perhaps the relationship is not as bad as they thought."

Since getting him to acknowledge those positive aspects is exactly what you're after, wouldn't you be foolish not to use memories of the good times to your advantage? You *can* help your man remember and reconnect; all it takes is a little thoughtful nudging.

"You know what I think it did for us?" says Sandra, a thirty-five-year-old accessories buyer from Dallas. "The thing that tipped the balance for Jim deciding to come home?"

It was the night we were having a drink, trying to decide what to do about my Toyota, which was going to cost more to fix than replace, and I started chatting about the trip we'd taken to Cabo San Lucas before we were married. We'd rented a jeep and driven along the deserted coastline of the Sea of Cortez—miles and miles of wilderness, empty white sand beaches, breathtaking mountains, bright desert flowers. We'd stopped to picnic, and then made love, naked, in a swirl of sea foam.

When I reminded Jim of this, recalling the most intimate details of our lovemaking, I could see he was ready to come back. It wasn't anything he said exactly, but the look in his eyes told me he knew he might be about to lose something wonderful, and he didn't want to do that. Sure, there was a lot of backing and forthing before he actually came home, but it was the reminder of the trip to Baja that turned the tables. I know it.

WHAT NOT TO DO: FOUR TACTICS SURE TO BACKFIRE

▪ *Don't panic.* San Diego marriage and family therapist Joanna Bitner says that it's *the* most common mistake spurned women make. "If, through sheer terror, you start pulling out the classic 'big guns'—using the children as pawns, telling them what a lousy father he is; initiating court proceedings—while you're still in the shock/rage stage, you could blow everything," says Bitner.

▪ *Don't threaten.* Don't say you'll withhold such resources as the kids, property, money, or to tell his employer and family what he's up to. Don't threaten to commit suicide (very tacky). Don't threaten, period.

▪ *Don't show any signs of weakness.* Don't show depression, other self-destructive behavior.

▪ *Don't be obvious.* Create a little intrigue, yes, but that doesn't mean meeting him at the door in edible underwear the first time he comes over to discuss your joint tax returns. Get subtle!

CHAPTER 7

Get Sexy!

One final step in your quest to get him back is so important, we feel it deserves a chapter all its own. That step has to do with sex. Whatever stage you're currently at in the reconnection process— starting to reestablish contact or on the verge of sleeping with him, feeling sexy about yourself is a terrific ego booster. It makes you attractive, not simply to him but to the world at large; it puts a sparkle in your eyes and a bounce in your step. The sensuality you beam out permeates every encounter, from the admiring, "Hey, baby!" you get from a cute hardhat (no, that's not always sexual harassment — said sweetly, it can be fun, and great for your morale) to the newly solicitous way your man helps you off with your coat when you're meeting for a drink. But you're not doing all this solely to win him back, or to seduce other men in an attempt to make him jealous.

You're doing it, first and foremost, for yourself. Why? Because having a secure sense of sexual self makes you feel good all over, inside as well as out—happier, earthier, more alive and in touch. At this point, you don't have to be having sex to feel sexy, but once you feel it, everything else will fall into place.

Certainly, if for years you've pushed this vital aspect of your being into a corner, it may take a little time to coax it out. That's why it's crucial to start *now,* so that when the time for sex is right, you'll be ready.

The problem is, at the moment you may be feeling a little wobbly. You know sex is a big reason men stray, and all along you have probably been picturing the other woman as an erotic genius—all black lace garter belts and high-heeled boots, plus a sexual repertoire that would make Sydney Biddle Barrows blush. Well, guess what? Many experts say the idea of the other woman as invariably sexier than the spouse is a myth.

"Since an affair involves sex, it is often assumed that the affair is about sex and that the other partner in the affair is a champion sexual athlete," says therapist and author Frank Pittman. "Of course, that is sometimes the case. But in my practice, I've noticed that it is about as common for the infidel to acknowledge that sex was better at home. And affairs may not involve very much sexual activity at all. Most affairs seem to involve a little bad sex and a lot of time on the telephone."

Be aware, too, that in cases where an actual separation occurs, many philanderers are stunned to find that the sexual kicks they got before the split suddenly fall flat. Partly, this has to do with a society that still doesn't encourage men to face or deal with their emotions the way women do. It seems to never occur to them that they can't walk away from a long-term relationship without feeling *something*—sorrow, guilt, confusion. But feel, of course, they do.

"Men are often surprised to discover the state of their emotional health has some impact on their sexuality," writes Susan Crane Bakos in *Dear Superlady of Sex (Men Talk About Their Hidden Desires, Secret Fears, and Number-One Sex Need)*. "A woman would know the sex is 'flat' because she really isn't ready to have sex yet. A man, on the other hand, believes he should always be ready to have sex—and, when he isn't, fears something is wrong with him."

For her book, Bakos sent out a questionnaire to which over 1,000 men responded, and approximately one-third said they'd had sexual problems after a breakup, from "the inability to achieve or sustain an erection to postcoital depression or vague feelings of discontent." But almost never, says Bakos, did they pay attention to the wisdom of the penis (which, through such second-rate performance, was obviously trying to tell them something). So don't assume that while your man was gone, he was having ten orgasms a night and doing wild stuff with Cool Whip. He may, in fact, have been in a lot more trouble than you ever were, so if anything, you have to feel a little sorry for him.

Raw sex isn't what men want most, in any case. More than anything else, they long for *affection* in bed. They want to be hugged, kissed, stroked, caressed—just as we do! Bakos, who's also been a columnist for both *Forum* and *Penthouse,* and writes often on sex, says the question men have most often asked her is, *Why doesn't she touch me more often?* "I've received more letters from men who want more touching, stroking, kissing, sucking, and loving than from those who want more of the exotic sex practices," notes Bakos. "About half of the men in my survey said they did not get as much reciprocal foreplay from their partners as they would like." For 80 percent, Bakos adds, the number-one complaint was women's passivity in bed, the assumption being that men don't need any preparation because they're always ready to perform.

Similarly, in his book, *Sexual Solutions,* Michael Castleman notes that "the widely held notion about lovemaking is that it is divided into three distinct stages: foreplay, intercourse, and afterglow. The very word 'foreplay' suggests that it happens before 'the real thing.' However, the idea that foreplay precedes actually 'doing it' is an indirect cause of many men's sexual difficulties. There are no such things as foreplay and afterglow. There is only *love-play.*"

Foreplay has always had a somewhat negative connotation: "It brings to mind the sex-manual blueprint for sex . . . as if making love were a game in which the major objective is to move on to the main event: Intercourse and penetration," says Shere Hite in the *Hite Report*.

Why do so many women assume that for a man, foreplay is not only unnecessary but undesirable? Bakos says it's a natural outgrowth of our belief that a man is ever-ready for sex. "We often treat him like an overheated motor on the verge of sexual explosion. If we fondle him too freely, he might reach orgasm 'too soon' or outside the vagina, which he 'shouldn't' do. Many women believe his need for more touching before sex indicates their lack of sex appeal. Maybe if we tossed out the word 'fore-play,' we would be less rigid about lovemaking."

Let's start by tossing out the *fore,* and keeping the *play*. You don't have to do things like tying him up with dental floss or licking honey off his knees (although if that's what he likes—and you're agreeable—those antics are just dandy). But you do have to get in there and play, love.

Good loving isn't quite as simple as scented candles, a little fellatio here, a little cunnilingus there, and how-about-if-I'm-on-top-tonight-dear? (although such elements may certainly be part of it). Basically, it comes about by being sexy, and that means liking sex. And when you like it, it shows—in the way you speak, move, laugh, touch, connect. Being sexy also means acceptance—of your body, of yourself as a woman. If you're obsessed with negatives (your bosom is less than bombshell, your derrière is more droopy than delicious), whatever your true erotic potential, you're not going to come across as sexy. In fact, an all-consuming concern about not living up to the American ideal—full breasts, long blonde hair, tiny waist, and so on—is probably causing you more problems than the "flaw" itself. Any woman who fervently believes she has to measure up or else is almost *inviting* rejection. Why? Because if you're forever worrying and comparing, you won't have a whole lot of energy left over for what you're after in the first place: hot sex. You'll also be more focused on yourself than on your man, and that never got a woman much of anything in bed.

Think about it. Many of the world's most gorgeous women—and that includes movie stars and other famous figures—are *not* sexy for this very reason. Oh, their lips are lush and their eyes are smoldering, all right, but instead of gaining confidence from their beauty, they agonize endlessly over supposed shortcomings (which may be as tiny as a broken fingernail) and thereby send out decidedly nonsexy vibes. It's women who are essentially happy with their looks (whatever those looks may be), and see themselves as alluring, who attract like crazy.

"Perfect" doesn't equal sexy, anyway. It's human *vulnerability*—hair ruffled by the breeze, a slightly lopsided smile, an endearingly stubby nose that attract, make people feel they can get through. Actually, female stereotypes of sexiness are changing. Many of today's top stars—Glenn Close, Meryl Streep, Susan Sarandon, Angelica Houston—are about as far from the old vision of seductiveness as you can get, but seductive they are.

Props won't do it, either. The slinkiest mini, briefest panties, all the kinky ploys in the *Kama Sutra* won't turn a narcissist into a siren. But if you allow yourself to be a warm, open, earthy, loving woman, you'll be sexy in a rumpled T-shirt and jeans.

Being sexy also means you're intensely aware of your body, from the very top of your head on down. As you stroll or lounge or even do the laundry, you have the buoyant, unerring sense that all working parts are *there,* and doing just fine. Everyone is born with this awareness, and if we were lucky, no parent ever said "don't touch," or in other ways made us feel our bodies were somehow digusting. Free to explore, we then delighted in everything from masturbation to the delicious tickle of a powder puff on bare baby skin. If you *weren't* among the lucky ones—and many of us weren't—it's this sense of awareness you want to recapture.

Sexy is being a little bit bold as well, and having a sweetly brazen air that says: "I deserve attention; I want to be noticed."

Finally, sexy equals giving. When you're happy with, and secure in, your own sexuality, you're free to revel in bringing your husband or lover to new heights of passion. And the obvious fact that you've given him pleasure further confirms your appeal.

Now for the big question: Can a woman actually *learn* to be sexy? Definitely, the answer's yes, and again, you don't have to be drop-dead gorgeous or have a body like supermodel Cindy Crawford's to pull it off. Everyone, however, flat-chested, near-sighted, frizzy-haired, or skinny, has a whole lot of temptress simmering just beneath the surface; all that's needed is the determination—and confidence—to call it up.

Before we go any further, it's important to note that some of you already may have slept with your man again by now; more of you have (probably wisely) held off. Exactly when you do sleep with him depends on your particular situation. If sex was a problem area in your past relationship (you turned him down often, criticized his performance, never wanted to try anything new), then sooner may be better than later. Trust your instincts on when; what we're concerned with here is how you *feel*.

Whether you've already done it, are about to, or think the big moment is still some weeks, or even months, off, the first time you two sleep together again can be tense. So much seems to hinge on it. If the earth doesn't shake, rattle, and rocket off, you reason, it's all over. Why would he want to stay with you when you've failed this initial, all-important re-entry test? Well, it might help to know that he's just as worried as you are—maybe more so. Keep in mind that while it's possible to fake an orgasm (we're not necessarily recommending it, just saying it can be done), it is very hard to fake an erection. Talk about pressure! Then, too, men feel more responsible for the success of love-making than women do.

Bernie Zilbergeld, clinical psychologist at the Human Sexuality Program, University of California at San Francisco, was talking literally about first-time sex when he wrote the following, in *Male Sexuality,* but the concept is just as valid for the first time the *second* time around: "Men have what they consider to be special concerns about first experiences. Since they believe they are totally or primarily responsible for the management and outcome of the sexual encounter, they wonder if they can get the woman ready, get and maintain their erections, and provide the kind of ecstasy they assume their partners desire. In short, they hope their performances will be, if not fantastic, at least passable."

Zilbergeld goes on to say that because of the tension that frequently accompanies first-time lovemaking sessions, they are often less than soaring. "Many men do not get or maintain erections in such situations or they ejaculate more quickly than they like, and then feel bad about these 'failures,' " Zilbergeld explains. "Other men function adequately but don't get enjoyment from the sex. Many women do not have orgasms the first time they have sex with a partner, a fact for which many men blame themselves."

"We'd been living apart for about five months," a thirty-two-year-old travel writer recalls.

And I was so petrified about being in bed with Ron again, after so long, and after all that had happened, I was actually shaking inside. But Ron seemed very cool, very in command, which kind of upset me. I kept thinking, "Hmm. Did he learn that from *her?*" I mean, he was coming on like this erotic *machine,* and instead of arousing me, it absolutely chilled me—all that advanced technique, and him saying, "How is it, baby? Is it good?" every other minute. It was like something straight out of a grade-B movie. But I didn't want him to think I wasn't enjoying it—this was my big chance to show him how hot in bed I could be, too—so I pretended I was going wild; you know, lots of moaning and thrashing around. I didn't have an orgasm, although, God knows, Ron tried hard enough to give me one, and although he finally had one himself, it took him an awfully long time to get there. But here's the funny part. Just when he was about to climax, Peter, the dog, who'd been hiding out the whole evening, suddenly raced into the room, growling and barking, and jumped on the bed. He hadn't seen Ron in a while, and was used to my being alone, so I guess he was trying to protect me. Well, it certainly broke the tension—imagine trying to finish off an orgasm with a hundred pounds of sheepdog-collie mix trying to bite your behind! Ron collapsed on top of me, with Peter on top of *him,* still nipping and growling, and we both started laughing.

When we tried again a few hours later, after locking Peter in the kitchen, the sex was much better. Ron later told me he'd pulled out all those technique stops because he was as scared as I as, and he thought a lot of action would blur the fact. Knowing that made me love him in a way I hadn't before. In the past, he would never have admitted to being afraid, and somehow, his having done so made me feel closer to him.

Remembering that your man is really concerned about his performance, and is afraid of being humiliated or found lacking (he's not sure what you've been up to during his absence, either, don't forget), should make you feel less as if you're on trial, and more as if you're both in the same boat—or rather, bed.

Why go to all this trouble? Why not just lie down, grit your teeth, open your legs, and be done with it? Because you'll be missing out on one of life's supreme pleasures, and that's a shame. What is even more important, sex can give you and your man more than just a fun time. When it's good, it permeates a re-lationship—strengthens it, heats it, holds it firm during times of stress. You can't just use sex to cement your union, though—you have to really want it—for its own sake. Again, to be sexy, you have to *like sex*.

Now, on to specifics, both big and small, on how to be the sexy, loving woman you really are.

WHAT'S SEXY?

▪ *Vibrant good health* is sexy (a blah, weary attitude toward love and life turns off just about everybody—men included).

▪ *Pricey lingerie* is sexy. There's something about sporting the wispiest of panties or a filmy bra that's marvelously ego boosting—even if you're the only one who knows you're wearing them. (Maybe *especially* when you're the only one who knows.)

- **Flirting** is sexy. Very sexy. In French, it's called *faire les yeux doux*—"to make sweet eyes"—and if you don't already know how to practice this age-old art, here's how: Lower your head, then raise it just a bit and look deeply into your man's eyes. Hold the gaze for a minute, then lower your eyes and look away. Repeat. It doesn't hurt to cross and uncross your legs here and there, either, or to lean forward while talking and lightly touch his hand to make a point.

- **Listening** is also sexy—and a big part of flirting. We've talked about it before, but nothing is more intriguing to a man than a woman who laughs at his stories, applauds his successes, commiserates over his problems at work—not in a phony way but because she really cares. Basically, flirting equals empathy with a little fillip of seduction tossed in.

- **A low, sweet voice** is sexy; whining screeching, mumbling are total turn-offs. If you don't know how you sound (and many of us don't), try talking into a tape recorder. A sensual voice is neither too high (as irritating as nails on a blackboard) nor too low (you'll put your audience to sleep). There are books and courses on how to correct voice problems, but the main idea is to breathe deeply from the diaphragm and aim for a tone that's in the middle range. Speak clearly, too—you want him to understand all those sexy things you're saying.

- **Smiling** is sexy—not high-pitched giggling or braying laughter, but a slow, sexy smile that seems to start somewhere in your soul and bubble on up.

- **A flash of lacy slip,** the outline of a delicate bra just barely traced through a white silk shirt are sexy. So are the sheerest of black stockings, perfume, fragile high heels.

- **An in-shape body** is sexy—not because it's perfect but because being fit makes you feel freer, more confident in bed.

- **Deluxe bedrooms and bathrooms** are sexy—and so pampering. You don't have to spend a fortune, either. In the bathroom, huge, plushy towels, a heated towel rack, fresh flowers, a delicate fern dangling over the tub help create a seductive ambience. Bedrooms can be country-cozy, starkly sophisticated, or that lovely old standby, ruffles-and-lace; the only vital point is to make this room *special,* a retreat from the rest of the world—no blaring TVs or worktables allowed.

All of the above should help you feel sexier about yourself, but eventually, you'll want to get sexy in bed. Maybe you're already an expert, and just need a little shoring up at present because you're nervous. Or maybe you'd like to be better at lovemaking, but aren't quite sure how to go about it. There are probably enough books on sexual technique to fill several hundred libraries, but one of the best we've found is the updated version of *The Joy of Sex,* by Alex Comfort. It contains not only easy-to-follow text but also drawings that illustrate just about every possible erotic option from the good old missionary position to love Indian-style (very steamy!). The very names of some of the "joys," such as Mouth Music and Love à la Florentine, are enough to make you feel wanton.

It's not as if you pick one option from Column A and two from Column B, and everything's going to work out sensationally, however. Would you believe it? There *is* no one "right way" to have sex! If more people were aware of this all-important fact, many of their sexual problems would go the way of the dodo bird. Some couples, once they've discovered the turn-on, can't get enough of it, whatever it is—smutty talk, a dash of mild s & m; others, after a trial run, are shocked out of their matching nightshirts. You have to do what pleases *you.* But you'll never find out unless you experiment. You also have to be aware of what's available; otherwise, you won't even know what to try. We therefore present a rundown on the most popular erotic choices, beginning with:

THE KISS

Slowly explore his mouth with your tongue—roof, insides of cheeks; entwine your tongue with his, then run it wetly over his lips. Don't stop at his mouth, either—let your lips play over his eyelids, neck, nipples, belly, palms, ear lobes, thighs, toes—anywhere and everywhere that seems to please him. Nibble occasionally; let him feel just a hint of teeth.

LOVE TOUCHES

Trail your fingers lightly over his buttocks, then in the crease; "walk" them up and down his body; brush them over the hairs on his chest, arms, legs, armpits, groin. Alternate with circling motions. Knead, press a bit harder to get his reaction.

ORAL SEX

Move your tongue over his penis with tantalizing slowness, lingering on head and rim. Lick. Suck gently. Cradle his testicles in one hand and you'll please him even *more*. When he's aroused, take his penis in your mouth and move mouth up and down the shaft in a rhythm simulating intercourse. When you sense he's ready to ejaculate, you can turn away and let him climax on your belly or between your breasts, or hold the semen in your mouth until you can discreetly get rid of it—but be aware that to most men, swallowing semen is a special gift of love. And how about giving *yourself* a gift, too? If you've never before suggested that he perform cunnilingus, maybe now's the time. Devotees say the sensation is unbelievable.

FANTASY

Does he dream of threesomes, ravaged ladies slung across his saddle as he gallops back to the Round Table? Whatever his fantasy, urge him to share it—and let him in on yours, too. You may not want to act on most such fantasies (couldn't, even if you did), but they serve a very important purpose: they arouse you, and fast. As author Nancy Friday notes in *Women On Top:* "It is fantasy's job to get us past the fear/guilt/anxiety. The characters and story lines we now conjure up make what was once forbidden *work* for us so that, just for a moment, we may rise to orgasm and release."

Do *you* feel guilty because you've been known to spend a steamy night with Kevin Costner when your man wasn't available? *Don't!* The fantasy, plus masturbation, helped keep you sexy, and even when he's back, you can still use it and anything else that heightens pleasure.

SEX GAMES

If you're aware of your man's fantasies (and you should be) such games might include bondage, spanking, playing governess and bad little boy—read some soft porn if you need ideas. These are just *games,* remember—nobody's supposed to get hurt. Also, if anything—even the idea of it—makes you uncomfortable, just say no. You can't have great sex when you're ill-at-ease or, worse, scared.

EROTIC TOYS

Choose from a lively assortment that includes everything from dildo-shaped vibrators to French ticklers to handcuffs lined with velvet. There are sex paraphernalia shops in virtually every large city, or you can send away. Some couples report the "plain wrapper" such toys come in is a turn-on in itself. For them, "taboo" equals "fun."

RAUNCHY TALK

You don't have to spew a stream of expletives—just try murmuring a hot word here and there.

DRESSING UP . . . AND DOWN

Take off your clothes slowly, item by item, and toss them on the chaise. By the time you're down to your bra, he should be wild with lust. Try leaving something *on* when you make love, too—a skimpy black garter belt you save for just such occasions, or black stockings.

WILD STUFF

Exotic new positions can indeed spice up your love life. You're not *obligated* to make love while sitting on top of your man, or to have a quickie halfway up the staircase, but these antics just might be a kick. Check out *The Joy of Sex,* the *Kama Sutra,* and/or other books on tantric erotica. For some reason, the folks in ancient India didn't have any dumb sexist hangups—Hindu ladies gave as good as they got. They were not only unashamed about assuming an aggressive role in bed, they exulted in it—and everybody had a fine old time.

Here, just to whet your appetite, is a fun tidbit from Vatsyayana's *Art of Love* (Book Two of the *Kama Sutra*):

> When a woman sees that her lover is fatigued by constant congress, without having his desire satisfied, she should, with his permission, lay him down upon his back, and give him assistance by acting his part. She may also do this to satisfy the curiosity of her lover, or her own desire of novelty.
>
> There are two ways of doing this, the first is when during the congress she turns round, and gets on the top of her lover, in such a manner as to continue the congress, without obstructing the pleasure of it; and the other is when she acts the man's part from the beginning. . . .

It's important to note that it's not just what you do, it's the way that you do it. (As Susan Crane Bakos puts it, oral sex "is more than licking him a few times as if he were a lollipop.") You can "kiss" your man's mouth, lips pressed tightly together, for all of two seconds, or you can let those same lips move sexily all over his body. You can "permit" him to videotape you dancing in boots and a G-string, or you can really get into it. The choice is yours.

High-quality sex also entails both love and feedback, comments Alex Comfort. Feedback means the right mixture of stop and go, tough and tender, exertion and affection. This sort of empathetic, caring sex, Comfort adds, makes us more, not less, receptive to each other as people. "This is the answer to anyone who thinks that conscious effort to increase our sex range is 'mechanical' or a substitute for treating each other as people. We may start that way, but it's an excellent entry to learning that we are people— probably the only one our sort of society can really use at the moment. There may be other places we can learn to express all of ourselves, and do it mutually, but there aren't many."

You have to realize, too, that although based on love, sex is very definitely a game—one in which you are sometimes aggressive, sometimes passive; pull back here and there to build desire. And you don't just do this in bed; you do it in life. To hold a man's interest, sexual and otherwise, you have to surprise him, keep him off balance, play him a little. So flirt, banter, drop male names, be unavailable occasionally—keep some erotic tension going. Remember what it was like when you two first met, and you pulled every trick in the book to get him to notice you? Pull those same tricks now, and add a few you've picked up over the years. To heighten desire, you have to understand the game— rule one being that men get turned on by *wanting,* not always by *having.* That's only human nature—and not just for men. Would you be so crazy about chocolate mousse if you had it for breakfast, lunch, and dinner week after week?

Right now, you may be thinking, "But I don't want to play games." Well, maybe. Psychologists Connell Cowan and Melvyn Kinder note, however: "Passion is and always has been a game.

Arousing and sustaining romance and passion in a man requires understanding how men operate and being willing to put your knowledge into action. You may choose not to play that game, but you will be missing out on a lot of enjoyment and fulfillment. Women who can periodically ration their needs for romance and learn how to build and sustain mild levels of uncertainty, distance and tension in a man get much more from men in the long run." Even that madeleine-loving traditionalist, Marcel Proust, once wrote, "An absence, the decline of a dinner invitation, an unintentional coldness, can accomplish more than all the cosmetics and beautiful dresses in the world."

One young woman who plays the game like a genius is a twenty-five-year-old associate fashion editor we know. Allison's face is lively and appealing, but not classically beautiful. She's on the short side, and curvy—far from cover-girl slim—but she works at her sexuality, revels in it, exudes it, and from the time we met her, has always had more dates than she could deal with. Then, last year, she started seeing Jesse, and everything changed— *this* was the man she wanted. When, ten months into the relationship, she sensed his interest was waning, here's what she did to get him back. Not all of us have Allison's exuberant self-confidence, but we can still learn a great deal from her gamesmanship:

> Jesse was very upfront—said he hadn't been sure for a while where our relationship was going, and admitted he'd met someone else. He didn't want to break up, he just didn't want us to date exclusively. Well, I wasn't about to give him up. I wanted him! So right away, I made sure he knew other men were interested in me. I flirted with his friends so they'd go back to him and say, "Hey, she's really hot! You'd be crazy to leave her." Or, I'd mention a cute new guy at the office, or leave my appointment book open on the table so he'd see other guys' names. I never lied— I actually had the dates. It was more to make sure he knew I had other options. Also, Jesse's the kind of guy who likes

to feel the woman he's with is sought after; I think most men are like that.

Whenever he asked where I'd been, I made it sound really fun. Instead of saying something like, "Oh, I just went out for dinner," which could have meant I had a pizza with three girlfriends, I'd tell him, "It was this formal dinner party some friends dragged me to; very European. I wore that black velvet you love, the one that shows a lot of cleavage." It was, true, too, so why not let him in on it?

Mainly, though, I reeled him back in through sex. Not to boast, but I've always been good at sexy repartee, presenting myself in a sexy way, so I just took that a couple of steps further. Like, we'd be at the movies, watching some steamy sex scene, and I'd lean over and whisper: "What do you think of that? Should we try that?" He'd want to race right over to my apartment, of course, but I wouldn't. I'd make him wait—a few days, even a week. Or, I'd mention a sex toy I was going to buy, and sort of taunt him, keep dropping little hints about this errand I had to run. "What is it? Did you get it yet?" he'd ask. And I'd say, "Not yet. When I have it, I'll let you know!" It drove him absolutely wild.

I tease a lot in bed, too. Jesse never quite knows what's going to happen next. We're always trying something new—otherwise, how can sex be fresh and exciting? I'll do anything . . . well, almost. But not always *when* he wants it. Or, just when he thinks we're going to have straight sex, I'll come up with something crazy, like this position I read about where the man is standing, and you're kind of in his arms, your legs wrapped around his waist. Maybe I keep him on edge, but hey—I got him back, didn't I?

Is this *nice*—all this teasing, withholding, seducing? Perhaps not. But you can be a good girl, or you can be good in bed — and keep him there. Also, remember you're not *only* playing; the very fact that you now have a life of your own is attractive, and by definition means you really *will* be distracted or unavailable at times.

Do be careful not to pull out all the stops until you see where your man is at, however. He may be ecstatic that you're eager to try oral sex or love in the shower, but if he remembers you as having been rather shy and passive in bed, he'll be petrified if he's suddenly faced with a wild woman. See how far he wants to go before you go all out.

One way to know how far he wants to go it to encourage him to *tell* you—and you tell him what you want, too. If you aren't able to communicate your needs, and find out what pleases him in the process, sex won't be the joyous, deeply gratifying experience it can and should be.

Many women still have a hard time expressing carnal desires— probably because, until recently, such statements as "I love it when you lick my nipples" were considered both demanding and unfeminine. (Women weren't supposed to have erotic longings, much less graphically spell them out.) But in bed (as in most areas that have anything to do with emotion), we have to be the ones to take the lead. As we've already said, men generally don't do very well when trying to talk about feelings. They may be able to recite the entire plot of *Terminator 2,* but they'll rarely come right out and say they'd like to have sex standing up, or have an urge to make love in the garage, without a little judicious nudging. Nor will they usually make an effort to find out what we're after.

It's a little bit our fault, because we women often send out mixed messages. We may think we're being clear, but, in fact, our signals are often misread because we're not specific. Say, "Let's do something crazy," and the next thing you know, he's tying you to the porch swing, in full view of the neighbors. But the good news is, there's an actual *language* of love, a way to ask for what you want (and discover his wants) without scaring him or turning him off. Ready to learn it? Here's a cram course.

BE DIRECT

You don't have to come on like a drill sergeant (left, left, right, left, halt!) but if you're going to enjoy sex, you have to convey what pleases you. And that means, no generalities—in bed, hazy comments are *out*.

To help avoid confusion, try putting your desires in the first person: "I like it when you give me a backrub before we start making love" "I need you to hold me and talk to me after we have sex" "I do better when you touch me gently." Phrase refusals sweetly but specifically, too: "I don't think I'm quite ready for oral sex yet, but maybe I will be when I'm comfortable with you again." By focusing on your feelings (and also keeping his hopes up), you avoid hurting *his*. This way, you're not insinuating that his technique is rotten or his performance is lacking; you're simply letting him in on what you want, and showing him you think he's more than capable of giving it to you.

The direct approach works when you're trying to get your husband or lover to open up verbally, too. Do remember, however, that this isn't the Inquisition—a little honey goes a lot further than intense prying. The very fact that you've made yourself vulnerable by talking freely should help him feel more relaxed about responding, but even so, proceed with tact. When you phrase questions, concentrate on those that call for a more exact answer than yes or no. Asking, "Does this feel good?" won't get you nearly as many reactions as, "Tell me what you'd like me to do."

KEEP IT LIGHT

However strong your emotions, never lose sight of the fact that despite all the heavy, soulful stuff the poets sing of, sex is supposed to be *fun*. And the less ponderously and pedantically you deal with it, the more fun you'll have. Sometimes, we get so obsessed with technique, performance, intimacy, and orgasms that the good-time part gets lost. Sex is also *funny*. Whether it's humans or animals going at it, the act usually involves a fair amount of grunting, sweating, and getting tangled up. (Ever seen two giraffes making love? If you haven't, picture it. The image captures the essence of what we're trying to say.) So go ahead and laugh (together, not at each other) if you fall off the bed during a particularly acrobatic maneuver, or can't go ahead with a fantasy. One woman told us she totally cracked up in the middle of a medieval extravaganza, and that it actually made the sex *better*.

Humor can also help if you fail to have orgasm or he loses an erection. You can't get as silly with a serious man as you can with a freewheeler, obviously, but a good belly laugh or two often does far more to ease a sticky sexual situation than a bunch of phony gasps and moans.

USE BODY LANGUAGE

Word aren't the only way to communicate desires. Back up verbal messages by using your hands, lips, legs—whatever's available. You might also shift your body a bit if he's caressing you in a manner you're not wild about; put your hand over his to keep it where it is; gently nudge his head lower if you want him to perform oral sex; lock him into a satisfying position as orgasm approaches; move your pelvis in a rhythm that makes him catch on to what you're after. Your body can say a lot if you'll only free it up. Keep in mind, though, that body language and words have to match. You can *say* you'd love to try anal sex, but if your facial expression is akin to that of a bank teller faced with a masked bandit and a scrawled note that reads: "Give me cash or I kill you," you can't blame your man for being confused.

COMPLIMENT LAVISHLY

You can use body language to back up compliments, too. When he does something you particularly like, wriggle, stretch sensuously, all the while telling him how much pleasure he's giving you. Never worry about piling it on too thick—there's not a man alive who doesn't revel in being told he's terrific in bed. You have to be sincere, of course—for your own sake as well as his. If you praise him for something you weren't pleased with, he'll continue to do it—which is *not* the idea.

Praise his body, as well. Every man has something appealing about him, whether it's a gorgeous Mel Gibson behind, muscular thighs, or a kissable neck. Again, be specific. "I love your hands; they're so strong and sculptured-looking," is far more flattering than, "You're cute."

Tell him you'd like compliments, too—especially when you excite him. That way, you'll know what to do the next time around. And around.

BE YOURSELF

How you communicate in bed will depend on the sort of person you are. Yes, you want to overcome inhibitions that cheat you out of pleasure, but trying for a total personality switch rarely works. If you're rather modest, you probably won't be comfortable with raunchy patter; also, because you're pretending, the words will come out all wrong. A more earthy, abandoned woman, on the other hand, will naturally be more explicit in bed. Finding your own style of communication takes a little thought, but once you've discovered the one that suits you best, you won't have to worry about what to say or how to say it—you'll instinctively know.

Your man's style matters too. If he winces at a four-letter word or recoils if you get physically graphic, pull back. Although it's true that some hot-blooded women have, by virtue of sheer sexual energy, turned a shy, cautious mate into a tiger, in general he's not going to become a whole other person anymore than you are. So you have to be empathetic, take his style into consideration.

GIVE HIM TIME

Finally, keep in mind that most men aren't used to talking openly about what they want in bed (or hearing their women talk about it), so getting him to be specific may take some doing. In an atmosphere of love, warmth, and mutual trust, he'll definitely come around—just don't rush it.

Everything we've said about getting sexy—from communicating desires to being aware of your body—should help you have orgasms (if not every time, at least often). On reason so many women seem to have trouble in this area is that an orgasm is both a big deal and not a big deal. It's nonsense to say orgasms don't matter, but the more you think about how much they matter, the less you're liable to have one. Also, masturbation's fine, but it's a lot nicer to climax while having sex with someone you love. It's even nicer for you both to climax at the same time. Not required—just nicer.

If you read all the stuff ever printed on how to have an orgasm, you wouldn't have time to have *sex,* so we're not going to go into every single option available here. One relatively easy way is to position yourself during intercourse so that the friction is heightened. In the good old missionary position, you can do this by putting a pillow under your hips, and, when he starts thrusting, drawing your knees up toward your chest. Or, you straddle *him*— many women say that being on top allows them to maneuver better. If you need him to stroke your clitoris during intercourse to bring you to climax, his hands will be freer if he's kneeling in front of you. Explore to find out what works best for you.

There seems to be endless debate about vaginal orgasms versus clitoral orgasms, but as long as whatever's happening feel good— and as long as you *have* orgasms—who cares what *kind* they are? Herewith, from Lonnie G. Barbach's *For Yourself: The Fulfillment of Female Sexuality,* a short rundown on making orgasm more intense:

1. Prolong foreplay by teasing, allowing genital tension to rise slowly and then maintaining it. The longer you're aroused, the more your tissues will be engorged—and the more sublime the release.
2. Concentrate on what *is* happening rather than what's not.
3. Breathe deeply. Inhale through your mouth and exhale through your nostrils.
4. Be more active—involve your entire body.
5. Make noises. Really let yourself *go*.

CHAPTER 8

Signs That

He's Ready

Signs that a husband or lover is doing some hard thinking about returning home are usually quite clear. And if you've followed our nine-step formula carefully, he should now be at that point, or close to it. Calls and overtures increase. He uses just about any excuse to see you, and some of them are rather poignantly inventive, like "We've *got* to sit down and figure out why Billy is so afraid of the water." (Forget that Billy is only three years old, it's the middle of January, and the nearest body of water is a hundred miles away.) He's less and less willing to leave after drinks or dinner. If he's still living at home, he's suddenly around a lot more than he has been over the past weeks or months, and seems happy to have it that way. He may be the one to start bringing up memories of the good times. He may hint that things aren't going so well with the girlfriend

and suggest a weekend in the country, "to see where we're at."
Or, he may come right out and say, "I was an idiot. I love you.
Please take me back."

The problem is (do problems in the quest to get your man
back ever end, you may be wondering? But really, you're almost
there), it isn't enough for your husband or lover simply to *want*
to come back. You have to be sure he wants to come back for
all the right reasons. Of course you love him; of course you need
him. But you've been through a lot, and aren't about to be toyed
with. You're a different (read "stronger") person than you were
when he left, and you have to be as sure as you possibly can that
his change of heart is for real.

It's not enough, then, for him to say he's fed up with the
other woman. It's not enough that he's miserable because he feels
the entire universe sees him as a bad guy. It's not enough that
he misses your cooking, his home, the kids (although these are
certainly barometers of what's going on inside him). In the final
analysis, he has to want *you,* the *new* you—wiser, sexier, infinitely
more independent. His desire and ability to approach both you
and the relationship on a totally different basis are the real clues
to his readiness. You don't yet have to spell out the terms of
what you hope that new relationship will be, but you do have
to sense he's sincere.

"To achieve a true reconciliation, both partners must redefine
the other person and the relationship positively," notes Diane
Vaughn. "Reconciliation is not simply a return to what used to
be. It is yet another transition, with its own costs." New York
psychoanalyst Jeanne Safer adds: "Your man's attitude is important. What does he have to say about what he's done? Does he
feel genuine remorse? Has he given any thought to why he did
it? Or does he simply say, 'It will never happen again, I promise
you,' and leave it at that? His own assessment of what happened
is a vital sign of whether or not he's ready to get back together . . . at least on terms you can accept."

Obviously, holding off when the man you love seems on the
brink of reconciliation is murderously difficult. You'll need to
summon up every ounce of willpower you've got. But if you

figuratively or literally collapse into his arms at this point, without knowing *why* he's done such a seeming about-face, you're headed for trouble. So try to forget your heart for now, and concentrate on keeping a wary little part of your head on red alert, antennae up, as you assess his true motivations.

Sometimes, that assessment can be tough, because he may not know his true motivations himself. He may think, for instance, that he wants to come back because he misses all the comforts of home, but what he really misses is you; he just can't admit that yet. Or, he may say he can't bear being separated from the kids, when—although the kids may be a big part of the reason—you're the person he can't bear being separated from most. You have to trust your instincts (remember that "inner voice"?) because you, after all, know the man better than anyone else—but the main thing is, however ready he seems, don't rush. This doesn't mean you should sadistically keep him dangling for a long period of time—if you do, he may just give up—only that you're clear about his feelings before you say, "Welcome back."

One relatively easy way to clarify the situation, suggests Jeanne Safer, is to ask a friend who knows you both well, and whom you trust implicitly, to feel him out. "Any man who wants to come back home will tend to give signs of that fact to others," says Safer. So get a handle on exactly what those signs *are* through feedback from a friend. If he or she reports that your man talks about you constantly, is always asking what you're up to, wants advice on how he might best approach you, or keeps wondering aloud how on earth he ever got himself in such a mess—start celebrating. These are all indications of good intent. If, on the other hand, he mostly moans about how strapped he is for cash, or how the Chinese laundry in his new neighborhood overstarches his shirts, or he complains that a business associate cut him dead when he saw him out with the girlfriend, best to wait until he gets down to the nitty-gritty—like realizing how much he loves you. Here are more signs that show he's ready, plus tips on what to watch out for.

HE'S WILLING TO HELP PINPOINT THE TROUBLE SPOTS IN YOUR RELATIONSHIP

This sign is truly vital, because if he's reluctant, or downright unable, at present to take a close look at what went wrong, nothing much is liable to change once he's back. Trouble spots don't have to be big time (such as lack of communication, inability to show affection); in fact, cutting problems down to size is usually better, because it reduces them to a level you can deal with. One woman told us that when she first started therapy after her husband left her for a twenty-three-year-old dancer, she'd go in dying to talk about overwhelming emotions—grief, rage, and so on—but could never get anything out. "Just tell me what you did this afternoon," the therapist would say. And, of course, the minute Valerie forgot about those huge, murky-gray areas like grief and began focusing on such specifics as, "On my way over here today, I passed the place in the park where we used to go on picnics when the children were little and I felt . . ." she got moving.

Few men are going to come bouncing in all super-verbal and eager to communicate their definitions of the relationship's shaky areas (sounds sexist, maybe, but it's true), so don't count on that happening. *You* are probably going to have to nudge your man into opening up; if you don't, you'll only be operating on guess-work—which leaves a lot of leeway for error.

The word *communicate* has been so overused, particularly in regard to relationships, that you may be ready to sign a petition to have it removed from the English language. There are books, magazine articles, and courses to help you learn how to express feelings; a whole new jargon has even emerged: "Thank you for sharing" "I hear you" "I know where you're coming from." What most of this stuff doesn't teach you, however, is how to get someone *else* to "share," particularly a man.

"Men especially are powerfully conditioned not to express their feelings," notes Cristy Lane in *How to Save Your Troubled Marriage,* co-authored with counselor Laura Ann Stevens. "Our culture has decreed that it is 'feminine' and 'sissy' for boys to have feelings. Parents of both sexes seem to encourage this. It is okay to have a tomboy daughter, but not a sissy son! Wives need to understand and be sensitive to the difficulty their husbands may have in discussing their feelings."

While it's true that times have changed, and that these days most parents *don't* think it's 'feminine' for boys to have feelings, we're assuming your boy is over twenty—which means he was probably raised to keep it all in, not let it all hang out. You therefore have to go out of your way to create a warm, non-judgmental, encouraging climate so that he won't feel threatened. Look at it from his side for a second: he's the one who strayed, he's the one who caused the trouble, and yet now he's expected to start pinpointing what else went wrong. In his mocassins, wouldn't you feel a little uncomfortable?

So, you don't start out hostile; obviously, that will make him instantly clam up. Instead, once he's agreed that talking over problems is a good idea, you might say something like, "Listen, sweetheart; it kind of drove me crazy, the way you switched on the TV every night after dinner. I know how hard you work, and I know you need to relax when you get home, but it made me feel as if you didn't know I was *there*. Now, I'm sure there were lots of things about *me* that made you want to climb the walls. You go first, and then I'll talk."

When he does start talking (which he will, if you phrase the invitation so gently and charmingly), for God's sake, don't get mad or interrupt him. You'll soon have your turn. Again, this is not the time to try to start drawing up contracts vis-à-vis your new relationship—pinning him down to promises about not leaving you with the dishes night after night or anything else. That comes later. Now, you just want to be sure he's willing.

HE SEES THAT YOU ARE A STRONGER, MORE INDEPENDENT WOMAN—AND LIKES WHAT HE SEES

This, too, is important, because otherwise, he's coming back on a fantasy basis. In many ways, you are a different person from the one he left (so, we hope, is he), and he has to accept and delight in that person if the new relationship is to work.

Separation does change people. "Living apart can itself bring about changes that leave both partners better prepared to interact: changes that, had they happened during the relationship, might have prevented all this," notes Diane Vaughan.

How do you know when your man is happy with the new you? Easy! You can see it in his eyes, his smile; you hear the pride in his voice when he talks about you to others. He'll encourage you in your career, support your interests. And he won't just be saying the right words—you'll feel that he really means it.

"It had always been a family joke that I couldn't drive," says a fifty-three-year-old librarian. "And, to be honest, it *was* a joke."

> I'd be mortified to tell you how many times I failed the test. But when Alan left, I had three choices: walk the two miles back and forth to work every day; ride my bike; learn to drive. Well, the thought of walking or biking in the winter, or when it was raining, didn't exactly thrill me, and besides, I was getting a little angry with myself. "Joan," I said to myself sternly. "You are going to make an appointment with the driving school tomorrow morning, and you are going to take lessons until you learn to drive well enough to pass that test." Before, you see, it was Alan who'd always tried to teach me. And although he tried to stay calm, I knew how frustrated he was getting because I still couldn't parallel park or back up without bumping into something. Sometimes he got downright angry, as if his

ability to teach me was being called into question. I had a feeling I'd do a lot better with a stranger.

The instructor was absolutely wonderful. I think there were times he'd have done anything to get out of the car—once, an ambulance came screaming up behind us, and I just threw up my hands and put my head down on the wheel; thank God for dual control—but he was *so* patient. And after a month of lessons, I passed, and then bought myself a little second-hand convertible. I don't think I'll ever be able to drive seventy miles an hour on an expressway, but we live in a small town on the end of Long Island, and I can get where I need to go—to work, to the supermarket. It's freed me so much, I can't tell you. Now I'm not at anyone's mercy—having to ask Alan or a neighbor to take me somewhere. I just get in the car and go.

Learning to drive might seem like a very small step, but it wasn't. There was something symbolic about it. Alan felt it, too. He saw me driving around with the top down one day when he was still living with the other woman, and I guess he couldn't believe it, because he called that night and asked what I thought I was doing, driving without a license. I said, "Oh, but I *have* a license." Those six words summed up an important change in me, and he must have felt it, too, because from that point on, he started calling a lot. Now that he's back, he's always telling people how wild and crazy I was to have bought a convertible. "I wonder what's next, skydiving?" I overheard him say to a friend, beaming all the while. That made me feel really good.

It was weird, but I think after he got over his wounded-male-pride phase—he hadn't been able to teach me to drive so I'd gone to someone who could—Alan was actually relieved. He's much rather see me as something out of an F. Scott Fitzgerald novel—you know, top down, hair flying—then as a wife he has to chauffeur all over town. And why not? It's more fun for me, too. Best of all, this new way of seeing me has carried over into other areas. He isn't so dictatorial; we go out together more often; we're planning a trip to Carmel this winter to visit friends. And it all began with my learning to drive.

Alan obviously liked the changes he saw in Joan—and showed it—but if you sense that *your* man seems uneasy because you're no longer as needy as you once were, or resents the involvement you now have in work or a hobby, or gets annoyed when you speak your mind in a way you never did before, don't push it. He may simply need time to get used to the woman you've become during his absence, which is okay—he has to develop a whole new set of reactions when dealing with you, after all. But if negative attitudes, subtle or otherwise, persist, his readiness is certainly in question. He may want to come back, all right—but to the life, and woman, he had before he left. Although there are indeed some rare cases in which couples were basically happy with both themselves and each other before the man strayed, and the affair was an aberration—like a flash flood, or a hailstorm in April—in general, a longing to return to the status quo is motivated by elements that have little to do with love. Rather, the urge to return comes from the discovery that the cost of ending a relationship is high. New, unforeseen problems—both practical and emotional—turn out to be staggering, and many men are not equipped to handle them.

"They are overwhelmed by the ill will of family and friends, the loss of other relationships, missing the other person or the home environment, or the guilt associated with causing others pain," explains Diane Vaughan. "The life-style they have opted for may be disappointing; the lover proves difficult or unfaithful; their income does not adequately meet their needs."

In his confusion and anguish, such a man will often make a big play to get back what he had before. That sort of motivation is far from positive, however, because it hinges on social and financial pressures. It's like wanting to have a baby because "everybody's doing it," not because you truly love children and understand that you're in for at least twenty years—if not a lifetime—of commitment. If your man begs for a reconciliation *just* because the going's gotten tough, and you're seduced into agreeing to it (the idea of a return to the status quo can be seductive to you, too), the odds are heavy it won't last, and you'll be right back where you started.

HE REALIZES THAT YOUR NEEDS HAVE CHANGED, AND IS READY TO DISCUSS HOW TO HANDLE THEM

Before Alan left, Joan may have needed a ride to work; *now* what she needs is a man who'll fix dinner and walk the dogs on the two nights a week she takes a creative writing course. Similarly, you once may have needed help in balancing your checkbook; *now* someone leaning over your shoulder, offering advice (or criticism), is only going to make you crazy. What you need is *space*.

It's hard for most men to relinquish control in such traditionally male areas as money, or to take on typically feminine tasks, such as cooking, so don't be discouraged if you have to nudge him a little at first. You almost *owe* it to your man to make it clear that life has changed a lot since he left, and there are a whole new set of needs waiting to be addressed.

Many of your emotional needs will have shifted, as well. In the past, it may have seemed cozy and comforting for your husband or lover to take you on his lap, pat you on the head and tell you not to worry—he'd take care of everything. These days, *you're* used to taking care of everything—or, at least, of yourself—so that pat is truly patronizing. You require mature, equal-to-equal feedback, not direction; you crave real talk, not just the old "how was your day, dear? Fine. How was your day?" ritual that once characterized your conversation.

Handling different needs (he'll have some too, of course, but you already know that) will obviously take some doing. The main point is to be sure he's open to it. Actually, he may be ecstatic that you no longer need him to change a tire or deal with the IRS, but want him for more fulfilling doings.

"When I told Paul that if we got back together, I really wanted more out of sex than I'd been getting, at first I thought he was going to have a heart attack," says a thirty-one-year-old makeup artist.

> He'd always thought I didn't want to make love because I was cold, or undersexed; he even had me believing it. It was only after we separated, and I started thinking about it that I realized very few women would want to just be, bang . . . uh . . . penetrated. I mean, the way Paul carried on—or didn't carry on—I might just as well have been a cored Granny Smith apple, or a mitten. I'm not out to be vulgar, but it's the truth. And if you want to know more of the truth, it wasn't just thinking that made me zero in on my needs. While Paul was gone, I had a short but very sexy affair with a hair stylist I met when we were both on a photography shoot. For a woman my age, I guess I was pretty naïve—I never knew that making love could be so fabulous. He wasn't the sort of man I'd ever want to have a real relationship with, but he sure showed me what sex was all about.
>
> I never told Paul about the affair, and I didn't harp on his lack of technique. All I said was that sex should be special, important, and that I didn't feel it has been that way for either of us. Well, after the shock wore off, he told *me* that he hadn't dared try certain foreplay or oral sex or any of the other great stuff because I hadn't seemed to *want* it. It's unbelievable, the stupid messes people can get themselves into when they don't communicate, isn't it? Anyway, from that moment on, Pual seemed in an awfully big hurry to come back home, and when he did, and we had sex together for the first time in months, it was better than it had ever been, and now it's better than better—it's fantastic.

HE'S CHANGED, TOO

He has to accept that you've changed, yes, but *he* has to have learned something about himself during the separation as well. Maybe living apart (and that doesn't have to mean physically; you may have been emotionally "apart" while still in the same house) has shown him how work-focused he was, to the exclusion of everthing else. Perhaps he now sees how limited a life without fun, friends, laughter is. He may be sweeter, more tender, less rigid. Whatever he is, he's *different*.

No one, your man included, is going to do a total personality switch, and if you think about it, you wouldn't want that to happen—there wouldn't be much of anything you loved about him *left*. Instead, a little distance has helped him go back to being the person he once was, or should have been, before *life* with its endless pressures and confusions, intervened. And *because* he's changed, he'll no longer have to define you or and your relationship negatively, which is what got him into the affair in the first place. "Now free to compare the new life with old on a more equitable basis, [he] may conclude that more has been lost than won," Diane Vaughan points out.

The affair itself has also changed him. Fantasizing about another woman—steamy sex, candlelight dinners, no worries—is one thing; actually *being* with a twenty-three-year-old airhead who thinks *Casablanca* is a trendy new Spanish club is another. We know you don't want to dwell on the girlfriend, and you shouldn't; just be aware that she's had at least one positive effect on what is to be your new relationship. She has helped your man come face-to-face with reality—to see who it is he really wants.

"If it took Jim's having an affair to make our marriage as close and rich as it now, well, I won't go so far as to say I'm *glad* it happened, but sometimes I do bless that silly woman," says a forty-four-year-old photographer. "Maybe we needed exactly that sort of jolt."

"For the first time, he started really enjoying the children," a thirty-seven-year-old social worker comments. "Oh, before the affair he loved them, provided for them, but I don't think he ever got much fun out of them. Even when he took them to the circus, or the ice show, it was more from a sense of duty than because he wanted to. Then, a few months after he left, I noticed that not only was he seeing more of them, but what he was *doing* with them was different. He wasn't just taking them on 'absent-father' outings, where all they had to do was watch the movie, eat the ice cream; he was listening to them, talking to them, interacting with them on a whole new level. He was beginning to see them as people in their own right, not just two *things* he'd had because that's what a married man was supposed to do. And I realized that some serious shifts in his thinking were going on."

"I knew how much he'd changed just by the way he touched my shoulder, or took a dish from my hand and dried it when he came over one night for dinner," a forty-year-old substitute teacher remembers. "It wasn't simply the gestures themselves, although admittedly, in the past they'd been rare; it was the feeling I got that they meant something. He wasn't trying to be this paragon husband just so he could move back in. It came from his heart, and I knew it."

Be sure the changes in your husband or lover come from *his* heart (if those antennae are still up, this shouldn't be hard). Even the best of men are capable of putting on quite a little act if they're motivated by negatives (the girlfriend took off; the walls of a one-room apartment are closing in). Then, too, while his spending more time with the kids is terrific—you always wanted him to be a more involved father—you have to be sure he isn't just playing the role to please you. (also, that missing the kids isn't his main reason for wanting to come home). You don't have to glare at the man suspiciously whenever a sign of change comes up—just keep an eye on him for a while until he's proved himself.

HE UNDERSTANDS THE REASONS HE HAD AN AFFAIR, AND WILL DISCUSS THEM IF YOU ASK

This is a little different from pinpointing trouble spots—which you do together—because his insights will have more to do with himself than with you. Also, the emphasis here is not so much on your future relationship as on the past one. He'll tell you how he felt before jumping into the affair, and try to describe his feelings, his mental state at the time. Obviously, it can hurt a lot to hear the man you love doing a rundown on the reasons he left, so you may not want to press him for too many salient details—in any case, that's neither desirable nor necessary. But the fact that your husband or lover *understands* why he did what he did, and is willing to share the reasons with you, is crucial; otherwise, he's liable to do it again.

His wanting you to know the reasons is a good sign. It shows he's aware of your fears that he'll repeat the performance, which means he's thinking of *you*. And if he's basically a good, decent, loving man (if he weren't, you wouldn't want him back, right?), he's not going to offer such assessments as, "You were lousy in bed; I had to get sex *somewhere*," or "All that weight you gained really turned me off." Instead, he will be sensitive to your feelings, avoid laying blame, but still tell the truth as he sees it. So even if it's painful, try to hear him out. If he knows he used the affair as an escape hatch because he was under horrendous pressure at work, then your knowing it too can only help. In the same vein, listening to him discuss his mid-life crisis in depth won't be fun, but you'll glean important pieces of information to file for the future.

"Ken said that all his life, he'd done what he was supposed to do," says a forty-three-year-old teacher.

> He'd gotten good grades, won a scholarship to college, majored in business because that's what his parents had wanted, bought a house in the suburbs, supported me and the kids. . . . And then one day—the same day a young

associate in his firm won a plum two-week assignment in Tokyo that Ken had coveted—he suddenly looked in the mirror and thought, "My God. I'm forty-nine years old, and I've never done one single thing out of the ordinary. I'm missing out on everything—travel, fun, real money— I'm missing out on it all." He didn't want to tell me how he felt, though; he thought it would only worry me. And there, right in the same office, was Diana—waiting to listen and soothe and shore up his ego. That's how the affair began.

Several times during the course of this painful conversation, Ken stopped, his eyes searching my face as if he were trying to gauge just how much grief he was causing me. Well, he was causing me grief—a lot of it—but no matter what, I was determined to let him go on. I told him I wanted to hear what had happened—*had* to, if I was ever to trust him again.

I think because I urged Ken to keep talking, he now shares a lot more of his feelings with me than he ever did before. He knows I won't fall apart if he tells me about a problem at work, or laugh about his fears of getting older. Now, he can come to me for comfort; he doesn't feel the need to seek out a stranger. He knows I want to hear.

HE FEELS TRUE REMORSE FOR WHAT HE DID, AND REALIZES HOW MUCH HE'S HURT YOU

His simply saying, "Look, I'm sorry. I *said* I was sorry, didn't I?" is not enough. If your man is sincere in his remorse—the "gnawing distress arising from a sense of guilt for past wrongs," as the dictionary puts it—he will convey that distress by treating you with the utmost tenderness. Compliments—real ones, not trite one-liners—and little gestures of affection are just two of the signs that show how much he wants to make amends.

In the beginning, he may overdo it a bit. That's okay—it will be nice for you to bask in all the attention and let some of your bruises heal. But if he's absolutely wallowing in guilt, and keeps *on* wallowing after the initial chest-beating session or two, that's not fair—you're then put in the position of having to comfort him.

"I finally said, 'Hey, whose party is this, anyway? *You* hurt *me*, remember?' " says a thirty-nine-year-old personnel director. "This was after a particularly wrenching outburst during which Nicholas had been crying and moaning that he was the most loathsome human being on earth and didn't deserve to *live*, much less have a wonderful wife like me. What I said brought him up short . . . and then we both started laughing."

"I pulled him out of it by agreeing with everything he said," a twenty-seven-year-old paralegal recalls. "*Yes*, he had some nerve for asking me to take him back. *Yes*, he'd made a total ass of himself. *Yes*, even his own mother was really to kill him. After a couple of days of this, I guess he got tired of focusing solely on his own feelings, and started thinking about mine."

HE FEELS A NEW RELATIONSHIP WITH YOU CAN WORK, AND IS EAGER TO GIVE IT HIS BEST SHOT

The eagerness with which many men approach reunion is quite touching. Once they're ready, they can't do enough or say enough to show how much they want to try again. In a very real sense, this *is* a chance to start over—and that's exciting. You're a new person in many ways, he's a new person in many ways, the whole thing begins to seem like another affair or—better—a honeymoon. Some couples reported that their first few weeks, even months, back together were, in fact, as romantic as jetting off to Venice or cruising the Caribbean. All this can be well and good— the thrill of rediscovery will get you both through some inevitably choppy waters. But do keep an eye on the man who's euphoric about coming back, because you want to be sure he's not just dreaming. If he remembers only the good times, and fervently believes that life will once again be perfect (as if it ever was—or is!) the second he moves back in, you're going to be operating on shaky ground. Even in the most idyllic of reconciliations, something's bound to go wrong. You're going to have PMS, the dog still hasn't learned not to chew up his slippers, the children are—children. If his expectations seem to be a compilation of the most saccharine episodes of *Father Knows Best*, with a dash of *The Cosby Show* (how *did* those two manage high-powered careers, kids, social life, love life without any visible household help whatsoever?) and some hot sex scenes from *White Palace* tossed in, what *you're* in for is trouble. He has to understand that "different" doesn't equal "flawless." Life will still be there to deal with on a daily basis.

Another type to look out for is the husband or lover who keeps reassuring you that you'll work out all your problems *after* you're back together—why wait when you're both on a reunion roll? Well, the reason to wait is that if you're not certain major problems have been resolved, it's very likely all the efforts you've made will have been in vain. Think of it this way: If you'd just lost forty pounds—lived on cottage cheese and slivers of water-packed tuna for what seems like forever—would a month-long chocolate orgy be worth it? You don't have to *trash* his dreams for future bliss—just gently convey that bliss is far more likely to be a reality if you do a little troubleshooting now.

If your man is showing all these signs that he's ready, you're on the verge of closing the deal. But before you jump in and start negotiating, here's a final reminder of what to keep a close eye on:

- He's a little *too* eager—in a big rush to reconnect.
- He's not just sorry for what he did—he's wallowing in guilt.
- He's operating out of such negatives as social pressures, money worries.
- He'll work on problems, all right, but after he's back.
- Problems? What problems? He remembers only the good times.

- He misses his old life-style.
- He expects to return to the status quo.
- The kids are his prime motivation for reunion.
- His girlfriend took off and he's lonely.
- You have the uneasy feeling he's not sincere.

CHAPTER 9

Closing

the Deal

He's ready. You know it. He wants to come back—and for all the right reasons. Now comes the truly tricky part. You both know your relationship is going to have to be different, so that this time around you'll avoid the problems that caused pain in the past. At this crucial point, you certainly don't want to badger him, or make angry demands, or try to punish him, but you do have to get a few things straight.

Knowing you're going to have to get your man to agree to some terms is both scary and unsettling. Silly as it may seem, you're probably feeling something akin to first-date jitters, even though he is the man you know so well, have so much in common with, love so much. Such nervousness is perfectly normal, but you can ease it by reminding yourself that:

- You are a warm, loving person and *were* able to get along without him.
- He is coming home of his own free will.
- He has chosen *you* over her.
- He is *still* the man you love, admire, respect, and trust (though that trust will take some time to restore).
- He's lucky to have *you* back, and knows it.

Okay, you're feeling stronger. You accept that you have a lot of power in the relationship, and that after all the ups and downs, it was finally your *love* and *power* that got him to return. You want it to be wonderful now. You realize that love is about acceptance, and know you can accept him fully for who he really is (not his recent behavior—just him). You also understand that needing him is different from loving him. You've got that neediness under control—most of the time, anyway. But although you're ecstatic to (almost) have him back, and are willing to give, love, open up to him as never before, this time you have to make sure you're starting out on very solid ground.

Judith Wallerstein, author of *Second Chances,* explained why some reconciliations are successful and others are not in an article called "First You Separate, Then You Reconcile—Or Do You?" (*Cosmopolitan*, March 1992): "I've seen couples separate and reconcile repeatedly, sometimes over a ten-year period. If the reconciliation is 'geographical,' couples moving back into the house or bedroom without any attempt to change their interactions, then it probably won't work. If the reconciliation is psychological, if the couple are really committed to sitting down together and seeing how they can change their behavior, then getting back together is probably a good idea."

So, reconciliation is going to require a new level of commitment on both your parts—a new way of dealing with each other—and now is the time to make certain he understands that, and is in agreement.

Many psychologists feel that before getting back together, a couple should draw up an informal contract—a sort of "you scratch mine, I'll scratch yours" list of promises. We're not so sure. Here you are in this fragile but exhilarating place in your relationship, and suddenly you both start acting like lawyers. It seems rather cold to us—somewhat calculating and potentially off-putting. If you're comfortable with the idea of a contract, then give it a try. However formal or informal your list, be sure to put all your requests in positive language. For example, when negotiating, instead of saying "It really make me mad when you don't come to bed before one A.M.," try, "I know you have tons of work to do after dinner some nights, but if you'd just come in and chat with me for five minutes or so before I go to sleep, it would mean a lot." Or, rather than, "It drives me crazy to have your mother come for lunch every single Sunday; she snoops around, even checks under the bed for dust," say, "How about if we take your Mom out for lunch on Sundays? I think it would be easier on her, and we'd all have more fun." (Okay, so it will be anything but fun, but at least you've put the request in a way that won't offend him, and is likely to get results once the promise is on paper.)

The biggest promise you're after, whether on paper on not, is that your husband or lover swears *the other woman is out of his life forever*. We feel strongly this should be an absolute condition for starting over. He knows the pain you've been through because of her (actually, because of him), and you must make it clear that you will not go through it again. Let him know you're not just tossing out ultimatums; you don't want to threaten him or make him feel guilty. But you simply cannot live in such a way, and he must understand that, and end the affair now if he wants to come back. There is no negotiating on this point—it's either yes or no. He has to know you're dead serious, and that he has no choice on the issue. If he's not one thousand percent sure he can give her up for good, then you don't want him— at least, not yet. "For good" means no midnight phone calls, no quick little lunches at the pub to see how she's holding up, no stopping by to drop off her Gucci scarf, no nothing, when it comes to her. It's got to be cold turkey, and that's that.

We don't for a minute suggest that you sound all hostile and huffy when you state this condition. On the contrary—be your best warm, loving, supportive self; make it clear it's because you love him so much that you can't bear to share him. Tell him you hope he feels the same about you (you know he does, but it doesn't hurt to remind him how painful the very idea of infidelity can be). Let him know he gives you more than everything you need in a man, and that you want to provide the same for him as a woman.

The next big issue to settle is how the two of you are going to learn to trust again. Tell him you feel you have a chance to make your marriage better than it's ever been. If he hasn't done so in the preliminary stages of "readiness", ask him to share, if he can, the reasons he felt drawn to another woman. Don't push—just help him see you want to know what he was feeling so you can make it better for him now. One of the best ways to encourage him to open up with *you* is to open up with him. Let him know what caused your coolness, or anger, or withdrawal, before he left; talk about what you felt you needed that you weren't getting. Promise him that any hurtful behavior on your part won't happen again.

All this may sound a little Pollyanna-ish, but we're convinced it's the only way to begin to restore trust. That restoration is the toughest job you have ahead of you, and is going to take time, patience, straight talk—and then more time. And more patience.

"Many people struggle with the question of whether it's reasonable to trust again after their partner has had an affair," says Peggy Vaughan, in *The Monogamy Myth*. "The somewhat ambiguous answer is 'It depends.' It depends on whether they know where they stand with their mate and know what's going on between them. It depends on whether they share their thoughts and feelings on an ongoing basis or whether they mostly have to guess about what the other person is thinking and feeling. The only way to avoid guessing about the facts is to know the facts."

Sharing thoughts and feeling is what honesty is all about. It fosters closeness and understanding, makes you both more aware of each other as people. And the more comfortable you two are with this openess, the less reason you'll have for mistrust. (When you are sure you'll be told the truth about whatever it is he's feeling—even if that involves worries about some aspect of the relationship, or fears about fidelity—at least you'll have the security of knowing where you stand.) You'll also be free to unburden yourself—to tell him how much the affair hurt you, or perhaps how, at a certain point, you weren't even sure you wanted him back.

"At first I thought, 'oh, God, why dredge up all that emotional stuff;' it's just going to cause a lot of trouble," says a thirty-four-year-old freelance stylist. "But then I thought, 'how can I take this man back if I don't? What kind of precedent would I be setting?' If I hadn't told Jamie that this time around, I wanted to know him, and that I could only do that by his telling me the truth, no matter what, I don't think we would have lasted a month."

We all know the truth can hurt, but much of the power of the truth has to do with how you use it. Being honest with your man by no means requires that you pull out all stops and deliver a vindictive, detailed account of how, while he was gone, you slept with a gorgeous man you met on a business trip, and it was "the best sex you ever had." That's not honest—just cruel. The reason to be honest with each other is to establish a new foundation of trust. If either of you is insensitive or malicious in the way you present the truth, then the whole purpose of candor is defeated. Your aim should be to create an environment in which you both feel secure, loved, valued, safe, and happy; use the "truth" in a way designed to threaten the other, and you both lose. Instead of creating intimacy, you'll crush it. Instead of building trust, you'll build up your man's defenses, and the distance that created many of your problems will resurface.

Remember, too, that if you and your man decide to make a commitment to honesty, *do not* punish him for the truths he tells you. Vaughan points out that "punishing [a] mate for telling the truth will almost surely put an end to any further honesty." If you're truly determined to change your relationship—to replace the old half-truths and white lies with gentle but real communication—the going may be a little rough at first. You're going to hear some things that may hurt. But almost every woman we talked with said the payoff, in terms of closeness, ease, and trust was definitely worth it.

Margaret, a forty-eight-year-old teacher in Royal Oak, Michigan, puts it this way:

> The night I asked Nick to tell me about his affair, at first, I thought I'd die. We'd been through so much by then. When he'd moved out, I was devastated, but then I finally pulled myself together, and got a job teaching history at the local high school. So by the time we decided to give our marriage another try, we really were, in many ways, different people. We knew we couldn't fall back into the old, shadowy manner of relating, so we both agreed to try to tell each other the truth—the whole truth—from then on.
>
> I wanted to know about the woman Nick had been with, and at the same time didn't want to know. Actually, toward the end, I'd had a detective follow him, so I knew more than I let on. But I'd never really heard any of the story from him, so I said I wanted him to tell me, in his own words—and although it wasn't easy for him, he finally did. Nick's a design engineer, and this woman worked for a man down the hall, who was a good friend of Nick's. The three of them would sometimes go out for lunch. Her marriage had come apart the year before, Nick said, and she was lonely—also, flirtatious, and a lot of fun. At this the point, I literally started to feel sick, but I didn't let on. I didn't want him to stop. I had to know. Anyway, he told me that one evening when I'd been in Chicago, visiting my parents, they'd had a few drinks, and then gone back to her place, where—Oh, God, I can hardly talk about it, even now—she'd got him into bed. No, that's not fair. Nick didn't say that. He obviously hadn't been all that unwilling. He went on to describe a trip they'd taken to Florida together. At the time, he'd told me it was a press trip, but of course, it hadn't been. And he talked about the relationship—how it had developed, and how he'd finally realized that I was the woman he really wanted.
>
> There were moments when it was all I could do not to reach out and practically strangle him, but somehow, I

managed to stay calm—partly because I kept telling myself that he was back in our bedroom, opening up like this because he wanted the past to be over. Resolved, accepted.

I also began to see that by talking about the affair, what Nick was asking from me was a new level of acceptance and understanding. You know, it's amazing, but for the first time, I felt as if we really did have a chance. We were both learning to be open with each other, and to be vulnerable, and even though what he was telling me hurt terribly, when he'd finished, I felt closer to him than I ever had before. I know that may sound like masochism to some people, but it wasn't. We'd both spent so many years playing cat-and-mouse, unconsciously moving farther and farther apart, that this was the first "real" conversation we'd had in years. Ironically, Nick's honesty about the other woman restored my faith in him. I *knew* it was me he cared about now, not her, and from then on, I felt I could trust him.

"Obviously, I wish Grant had never had an affair," adds a forty-four-year-old book critic. "But he did. And if it had to be, I'm so glad I forced him to talk about it. Playing ostrich would only have diminished me as a person. What would I have done—suffered silently like some poor wife in a Victorian novel? Pretended everything was fine? Hey—I'm worth more than that."

So, the truth becomes the pathway back to trust. It may not be a direct route—there may be obstacles along the way—but based on the experiences of virtually all the men and women we talked with, honesty is the only answer if you want to begin to rebuild the trust that's been so badly eroded.

What else are you going to need? Faith—in yourself, in your man, in the relationship. It's not going to be easy to avoid that familiar panic the first time he's late coming home from the office. But is it worth shaking your newfound trust over what's probably nothing more than a traffic tie-up? Keep reminding yourself that this relationship means a lot to your husband or lover, too; otherwise, he wouldn't be back, and making so many efforts to change what was wrong. He wouldn't be the man you *love*.

Changing what was wrong with the relationship also means you each have to face your own demons—pinpoint what may be wrong with you (irrespective of your partner) and then assume responsibility for those problems. It takes courage to "stand alone" in such a way, but the very fact that you two were apart for a time should give you a big advantage. Why? Because you've both had time to think—see yourselves as separate human beings, stop blaming the other for everything from career troubles to mood swings. (And don't feel that just because he was seeing someone else, he didn't engage in some heavy soul-searching, too.) Separation forces most people to take a cold, clear look at themselves—and learn from the experience. Is it painful? Yes. But therein lies its power.

Sara, a forty-year-old head of a public relations firm in Phoenix, Arizona, told us the following story, which illustrates with poignant clarity what facing your own demons is all about:

> After Charles got involved with a woman in his AA group, I almost broke down—me, the stong one in the relationship. It was pretty ironic. I'd be in a meeting, and could barely keep myself from bursting into tears—pretty embarrassing when you're trying to explain to the staff that they can't let personal problems interfere with performance.
>
> Then, one weekend, I didn't get out of bed at all. And on the days I managed to get through work all right, I'd come home, crawl back into bed, and sob. This went on for weeks. I kept telling myself that I'd been the ultimate martyr all those years Charles had been drinking, and now this. Hadn't I been the perfect wife, always there to drive him home from parties? Always ready to help him to bed on nights when he'd collapse after dinner?
>
> And then it dawned on me. I hadn't been such a perfect wife at all. What I'd really always been ready to do was subtly remind him, over and over, what a disappointment to me he was. And then, when Charles finally gave up drinking, my role was threatened, and I panicked. I resented his going to AA, made fun of it. I was cruel to him more

than I like to admit. No wonder he'd turned to someone else—a woman who was supportive of the struggle he was going through. I saw that I was no pillar of strength myself, and that in many ways, I'd actually used him to make me appear strong to the rest of the world.

One evening, when he came over to pick up some of his things, I asked him to have a cup of coffee with me, and told him what I'd figured out about myself. He was truly touched—and said he knew what he'd put me through, too, with his drinking, and then the affair. We wound up in each other's arms that night, crying, and it was as if we were crying for the people we'd been, and the kind of marriage we'd never had. But soon after that, Charles came back home, and the incredible part is that our relationship really has changed. I've finally realized it doesn't make that much difference how the world sees me. What makes a difference is how I see myself. I'm strong in some ways and vulnerable in others, just as Charles is. We accept that about each other now, and it's made a huge difference in our marriage.

Facing demons. Honesty. Being certain the other woman is history—these are the main issues to get straight when you're closing the deal. But what about the little things? There are dozens of ways to improve your day-to-day life together—small efforts that, taken singly, seem trifling, but when totaled add up to a formula that can eliminate monotony and lack of connection—two big reasons men stray. Here are some of the "deals" that helped eight of the couples we talked to.

"WE AGREED TO GO OUT FOR DINNER ONCE A WEEK—JUST THE TWO OF US."

"I know it doesn't sound like much," says Jenny, a thirty-four-year-old bank teller from L.A., "but I used to come home exhausted every night, and then have to cook for Mike and the kids."

Sometimes it reached the point where I almost couldn't stand it anymore. Jimmy and Lori were often cranky, and demanded all our attention, so Mike and I never really had a chance to talk about anything important. When he was about to come home, at first, I wasn't going to say anything—it was like, "lets not rock the boat; the man's not even back yet"—but then, I thought, "No I don't want this new relationship to be the kind where I'm afraid to say anything for fear he'll leave again." So I told Mike how I felt, and right away, he suggested we make a ritual of going out alone together once a week. It's made such a difference, I can't tell you. Sometimes I feel as if we're dating again. We don't go to expensive places—we can't—but after a tough day, even Larry's Diner seems like Spago—especially when the alternative is cooking for grumpy kids at home.

"WE MADE AN 'OOPS' PACT."

"Here's how it works," says Margie, a fifty-two-year-old house-wife from Fond-du-Lac, Wisconsin.

Whenever either of us notices the other is reverting to the same old patterns, the other just says "oops." Then we stop, sometimes in mid-sentence, realize what we're doing, smile, and start out on a new track. For instance, it used to drive me wild when I'd have breakfast all ready on Sunday morning—eggs over easy, sausages, muffins, the works—and he'd say, "Just a minute, dear." Ten minutes later he'd *still* be futzing around in the bedroom and I'd just go crazy. But now, instead of yelling, "Richard! I've spent forty-five minutes fixing this damn breakfast for you; now get the hell in here and eat it," I call out, "oops" and he laughs and comes right in. It sounds like a little thing, doesn't it? But it really helps.

"WE TRADE TIME."

"Jim and I both felt our life together had been getting pretty claustrophobic in the days before we agreed to a trial separation, and we didn't want it ever to be that way again," says thirty-eight-year-old Sally, a reporter in Orlando, Florida.

I'd always resented it when Jim played squash after work and didn't get home till eight. And he admitted that it used to annoy him when I'd ask him to watch the children on Saturdays so I could do any shopping and errands I hadn't had time for during the week. It's not that he minded staying with them, but he has a demanding job, too, and he said Saturday was *his* only time to get anything done. So before he moved back, we decided to make a deal. Each of us would have up to six hours of free—meaning non-working—time per week. We'd be flexible about how to use it, and pitch in for the other during those hours. Now, if Jim want to play squash three times a week at two hours a shot, that's cool by me, because if I want to shop for six hours straight, *he* doesn't mind. It sounds sort of formal, but it works for us.

"WE COUNT TO ELEVEN."

"Hackneyed, I know," says twenty-nine-year-old Frances, a real estate broker in Princeton, New Jersey, "but Jay and I vowed to count to eleven each time we felt the impulse to lash out.

I used to be the guiltiest one—whenever something bothered me, I think I secretly blamed Jay and would just start attacking rather than thinking it through. Now, I start to count, slowly, and by the time I'm finished, I often realize it's not his fault that I'm frazzled, and the table's not set, and the kids have left their parkas in the middle of the kitchen floor. So why yell at him? Instead, I tell the kids to pick up their own parkas, and ask Jay, nicely, if he'd mind pouring me a glass of wine and setting the table. He counts to eleven instead of snapping, too. We've even got the kids doing it! These days, it's a lot quieter at our house.

"WE MAKE EACH OTHER FEEL GOOD."

"Just before we got back together, I figured out something very important," says forty-one-year-old Chris, a social worker from Evanston, Illinois.

Actually, it was advice given to me by a close friend. She said, "if you're the one who makes him feel good about himself, he'll never want to leave you again." Beautiful. Simple. Why hadn't I ever thought of it? So, what I try to do now is accentuate the positive, look on the bright side— all those clichés they write the songs about. I decided to try this on my own first, just to see what would happen, and—you guessed it—it brought out the best in him, too. I hate to say it, but I used to be openly critical of Phil, and now I just don't do that anymore. Sure, there are things about him that bother me, but I remind myself that nobody's perfect, and besides, after all we've been through, I really do appreciate him more than ever. He appreciates me more, too. And the deal is, we both let each other know it.

This comes out in little ways. Phil recently lost his job, and I was borderline hysterical for a couple of days. I'd look through the want ads and circle those I thought were right for him, offer to type up résumés—the tension between us was getting really bad. But then I remembered our pact and snapped out of it. Phil didn't need a mommy-schoolteacher figure; he needed me to help him feel good about himself. So I stopped "helping" and forced myself to be cheerful and upbeat. The poor man was having a tough enough time already without my contributing to his problems. My acting confident and unpanicky made him feel he'd soon find something, and in fact, he's lined up some promising interviews and is very optimistic. He also never fails to tell me how much my confidence in him means—which makes me feel good.

"WE JUST CALL TO SAY 'I LOVE YOU.' "

"Don and I started going to a marriage counselor right after he came home," Mary, a forty-six-year-old investment consultant in Charleston, South Carolina, remembers.

She suggested we say "I love you" to each other twice a day, even if there was a hurricane in progress, or the house was burning down. It sounded ludicrous to us, but since we were paying all that money for professional advice, we decided to try it. Well, believe it or not, it worked beautifully. At first, we both felt silly and self-conscious, but after a few days, we got into the swing of it, and saying those three little words became very natural and reassuring. It's so easy to assume your partner knows how you feel about him when maybe he doesn't. Why not use this simple method of telling him? It's the quickest way to show love I know of, and defuses a lot of the old volatility that used to get us into so much trouble.

"WE SURPRISE EACH OTHER."

"John and I agreed that once a week, we'd each try to dream up a surprise for the other," says Rachel, a twenty-eight-year-old New York City copywriter.

Nothing elaborate—we'd just think of a little gift, or an idea about some activity, and it did great things for us. One week, I bought him a tie with sailboats on it—John loves to sail—and he suggested we spend Sunday afternoon browsing around galleries and antique shops in the Village. I love antiquing, and he'd always seemed bored by it, so the very fact that he'd suggest it made me feel secure in his love. Another week, he bought me a big jar of red jellybeans—my favorite—and after work I surprised him at his office and took him out to a nearby pub for a drink. He loved it; said he enjoyed this particular surprise so much, maybe we ought to do it every evening. So far, my best surprise has been the kitten he brought home a few days ago. My cat died last year, and I had a really hard time getting over it. I couldn't believe John was capable of so much empathy—an animal lover he's not, and he used to sort of laugh at how attached I was to Tom. This surprise business is starting to bring out the best in both of us, plus, we're having more fun than we've had in a long time.

"WE FOUND A COMMON INTEREST."

"I used to feel hurt when Bob spent weekday evenings at the office, and weekends either at the track or glued to the TV, so this time around, I came up with a plan," says fifty-one-year-old Barbara, a literary agent in San Francisco.

"Why don't we find a joint project?" I said. "Something we can really get into and work on together." Bob was agreeable and we'd both dabbled in photography in college, so we decided to try that. We dusted off our cameras— actually, I bought a new one, since mine was practically vintage—enrolled in a course, and set out. We were especially interested in landscape photography, so we'd sometimes get up at 4:30 A.M. on weekends to catch dramatic sunrise shots. Or, we'd go on field trips, with no particular destination in mind—just drive in some general direction, stopping when the light was good, and pulling into a country inn or motel when it began to get dark. Having a joint project did wonders for our relationship, and it wasn't long before we started getting pretty good at photography, too. Bob even won a contest last summer. He's rarely at the racetrack these days, and his television time has gone way down, as well. I suspect he was using racing and TV as escapes; now, he seems much more comfortable with himself, me, and life in general. Photography really saved us— well, helped save us. I recommend figuring out something you both like to do—and then *doing* it—to any couple in the delicate process of putting a relationship back together. It's gratifying, and fun, to be working on the same thing at the same time.

Ten Men

Tell Why

They Strayed,

Why They

Came Back

When we contacted men who'd left their wives or girlfriends, and then returned, we were surprised at how eager they were to talk. Whether we met them in person, or just listened over the phone, their words spilled out, as if they had been longing to tell someone what had happened, so they could try to make better sense of it. We rarely had the feeling that any of these men were headed for another affair. They seemed genuinely sorry about the pain they had caused, and were much more focused on making their primary relationship work than on ever again seeking satisfaction outside of it. For this chapter, we chose the ten men we felt best expressed the confusion and searching an errant husband or lover goes through. Their stories are funny, and touching, sometimes awful, and very, very human. Hearing them may help you understand your man better—and forgive.

PHIL IS A TWENTY-NINE-YEAR-OLD BROKER WHO LIVES WITH HIS WIFE, SHERRY, IN VALLEY COTTAGE, NEW YORK. THE COUPLE HAS BEEN MARRIED SIX YEARS. THEY HAVE ONE CHILD.

I left because, from the moment we were married, I became an unpaid escort service for weddings, funerals, visits to hospitals, old folks homes. . . . The family was like a goddamn tribe. Every day, Sherry was on the phone with her mother and three sisters—the mother had this really cute trick of doing an emergency disconnect when our line was busy, which was just great when I was talking to a client. Besides the immediate family—the four girls and mommy and daddy—there were aunts, uncles, cousins, nieces, nephews, grandmothers, grandfathers. There was no time for *us*. Particularly, there was no time for *me*. We went to her parents' house for dinner every single Sunday; we took vacations with her sisters and their boyfriends or husbands. Every single social thing we did involved her family. I began to feel as if I were being eaten alive, swallowed whole.

One day, we had a big fight about never spending any time alone together, and I made such a scene Sherry agreed that the following Saturday, we'd take a picnic and drive up into the country, just the two of us. But then, of course, that morning her mother called up, frantic, to announce that Aunt Louise had been rushed to the hospital, and was about to have a hernia operation, so we'd better get over there fast. I didn't even know women got hernias, but in that little group, anything's possible—as I should have been well aware. So there we all were, clustered around Aunt Louise's bed, and at one point I went over to the window and looked out—it was a beautiful day, I remember, sunny and clear, and couples were lying on the grass in the little park opposite the hospital, holding hands, kissing, and I thought: "What am I doing here, in this room that smells of disinfectant, listening to lunatics talk about hernias and hysterectomies?" "Enough," I said to myself. Just "enough." Conveniently, three days later, I met Emily.

Emily's family was three thousand miles away; maybe that's why I chose her. She was easy and funny, but also very much her own woman. She lived alone in a one-bedroom apartment on East 89th Street, which was done all in white, and she liked the way she lived. She was a broker, too—very ambitious—and any thoughts of marriage or children were years away. I came up with all sorts of excuses so that I could spend time with her—working late was good; so was having dinner with clients.

More and more, Sherry went to her tribal rites without me, and it seemed to me, she barely noticed I was missing. When I told her I was leaving her, though, you'd better believe I got her attention. Suddenly, she was all over me—clutching, begging, crying, saying she couldn't live without me. I said, "Well, I can't live with you the way it is. I don't feel like your husband. I feel like this *thing* that's on hand to take you to weddings. You don't need me—you could hire somebody, or blow up a Ken doll and let him take you around." Between sobs, she said it was only normal for her to want to keep in touch with her family, and that I didn't understand because I'd grown up in a single-parent home—my Mom and Dad had got a divorce when I was seven. "Sherry, it isn't normal," I said. "And if you want to hear a real cliché, it's either them or me. Anyway, I'm not even sure if I want to be married to you anymore. I've met a woman who wants to be with me for my own sake, and you know what? It's a very nice feeling." Then I turned on my heel, just like in the movies, and was out the door.

I don't know what Sherry did or said to her family after that, but the next week, she called me at work and said she had to see me. We met in a little bar we used to go to when we were dating, and she looked great—gorgeous, in fact. The minute we sat down and ordered drinks, she took my hand and told me that from now on, I was first in her life. No more twenty phone calls a day. No more hospitals. No more emergency disconnects. And since that night, that's exactly the way it's been. Oh, we see her family occasionally, but that's it. Whenever any of them start to do a number on her, she freezes. I was particularly proud of her right after the baby was born. Her mother was all set to move in with us and stay for two weeks—or, probably, forever—

and Sherry said, very sweetly but firmly, that I'd already arranged for a nurse to sleep in, and wasn't she lucky to have such a wonderful husband? Hey, I felt ten feet tall, just the way Emily had made me feel, but better. Because I'd never been in love with Emily. I really loved my wife.

MICHAEL IS A THIRTY-EIGHT-YEAR-OLD SALESMAN WHO LIVES WITH HIS WIFE, LYNN, IN DES MOINES. THE COUPLE HAS BEEN MARRIED SEVEN YEARS. THEY HAVE TWO CHILDREN.

I travel a lot in my work, so affairs have always been easy for me. It's no big deal as far as I'm concerned. I think most guys screw around, or would if they had the opportunity. You know why I think guys screw around so much? It's because they like the action, the feeling of being in control, and all this psychobabble about intimacy is a lot of crap. I would have gone on that way forever if my wife hadn't told me she was onto me, and that if I didn't stop, that was it. I keep telling her it has nothing to do with her, but she's not having any of that, so now we're seeing a counselor.

The way I see it, if you can find a woman who likes the life you give her, who's good with the kids, who's up for sex whenever you're around, that's about the best anyone can hope for. Leave my wife? Never. What for? As long as she doesn't get too bitchy, doesn't nag too much about how much time I spend away from home, she'll do just fine. Listen, in other countries this kind of thing goes on all the time. What do they call it in France, when everybody goes off in the afternoon and has a quickie—*cinq à* something? I mean, what's the big deal?

In a funny way, I'm monogamous. It seems much sicker to me to keep breaking up families, the way they do in this country, than to do what you want on the side and keep your marriage intact. There's a couple we know that split up over the man's affair two years ago. They share custody of the two kids. Now they're each married to somebody else who's also divorced and a parent; between them, altogether they have something like seven kids, all running back and forth between families. Is that so good? I just don't get it. But I know my wife really means what she's saying. Also, she went totally nuts when she found out—started throwing things at me, trying to scratch me . . . there's a big dent in one of the pots hanging on the kitchen wall; it just missed my head and crashed into the refrigerator. Yeah, frankly, I'm a little afraid of her, if you want to know the truth. Also, I don't want to lose her. So I'm trying to see it her way.

CHARLIE IS A THIRTY-THREE-YEAR-OLD ASSOCIATE EDITOR OF A TRAVEL MAGAZINE WHO LIVES WITH HIS GIRLFRIEND, JENNIFER, IN BOSTON. THE COUPLE HAS BEEN TOGETHER SIX YEARS.

We started living together when I was only twenty-seven, and I think that was part of it. I'm a man who loves women. They're more fun to be with than men, more open, more interesting. Also, I'm a massive flirt—always have been, always will be. Before I met Jen, I was used to having a lot of women around—not just for sex, but because I really enjoy their company. I liked my independence, too. So right from the beginning, I was a little wary—not that Jen ever pressured me to move in with her. Actually, it was probably more my idea than hers. She just knocked me out, she was so smart and funny, and she knew all these talented people. But after three years of constant togetherness, I kind of felt the walls closing in.

Jen's hardly your typical wife type—she's a well-known writer, into the feminist movement—but even so, she was getting a little territorial. You know, like, "Do you realize you didn't look at me the entire evening, you were so busy coming on to so-and-so?" Also, she's seven years older than I am, and her life was more settled than mine had been. She wanted to eat real food, on plates, at definite hours; when it was my turn to change the sheets and I forgot, which I invariably did, she'd be really annoyed. But age aside, I think women have much more of a nesting instinct than men. Men don't make very good domesticated creatures, and the more women try to turn them into something they're not, the more it doesn't work.

Another thing—sex with the same person, even someone as good as Jen is in bed—gets boring after a while. There are only so many ways you can do it. So between the territorial business and not being allowed to blast music till four A.M. and have a burrito for breakfast if I felt like it, I was getting fed up. I didn't want to break up exactly; I just wanted some time off. So when this press trip to Aruba came up, I jumped at the chance.

It was on the trip that I met Angela. I'd noticed her on the plane right away—tall, about my age, with lots of curly red hair and a wide, sexy mouth. She wasn't pretty, but she had a real look. That evening, nothing was planned for our group, so after I'd showered and changed and had a couple of beers in the room, I went down to the bar by the pool. The sky was unbelievable, streaks of dark pink and gold, and lights were going on all over a big cruise ship out in the water. Angela was sitting at a table alone, and I asked if I could join her. She said yes, and that was it. We slept together that same night, but it wasn't just the sex; I really liked her. I can't sleep with a woman I don't like, and that's the truth. Still, I knew very well that if it hadn't have been Angela, it would have been someone else. I was ready.

Right before we got into bed, I thought of Jen, and of what we had together, and of what sleeping with Angela might do to the relationship, but then I suddenly had this vision of myself on the plane going home: It had lost an engine, it was clear that we were going to crash, and I kept thinking, "Jesus, I wish I'd had sex with her. Now I'm going to die and I didn't have sex with her." So I had sex with her.

We had five unbelievable days in Aruba. It was the ideal press trip—all you really had to do was show up for dinner. Otherwise, the time was your own. We swam and snorkeled and drank rum drinks and lay in the sun. Of course it was unreal, but so what? Reality gets boring, day in and day out.

Angela and I separted at the airport— she lived in New York

and I was going on to Boston—but we exchanged office phone numbers and arranged to meet in two weeks. I didn't know how I was going to pull the whole thing off, but I knew that I wanted to.

The same evening I got back, Jen asked me straight out if I'd been with someone else. As you can see, the lady knows me very well. We'd always had this deal that if either of us asked a direct question of that nature, we wouldn't lie. So I told her, yes, I'd met somebody. Jen was very cool—acted as if she didn't feel like pursuing the subject at any great length, just asked me what I wanted to do. I said I didn't know, but that maybe we'd better take some time off from each other. And she was like, okay, fine, if that's what you think. She watched me pack, and that was pretty much that. No hysterics. No how-dare-you's. I moved in with a friend who needed a roommate, and for about three months, I saw Angela almost every weekend. Sometimes she'd fly up to Boston, but more often, I flew down to New York. But I also stayed in touch with Jen. She'd call, or I'd call, and we'd meet for a drink or for dinner. She didn't dwell on what was going on, but once in a while she'd say something like, "Are you allowed to blast the Grateful Dead all night now, dear? Hmm. Guess so. You're looking a little . . . wan." But she didn't say it in a mean way—more like funny.

It was weird, because we never actually discussed the situation or decided anything, but after a while I was seeing Jen a lot more than I was seeing Angela. The distance thing was part of it, but in essence, I gravitated back to Jen because I like the person. I still haven't met anybody I like better, right or left. Maybe she's spoiled me. We have this little joke that when it comes to women, I've got a five-book minimum, and Jen's the only one I've ever met who's published five books. Also, I'm not real big on insecure women. I like strong women. I don't like women who bat their eyes and say whatever you want them to say. I like a woman who doesn't take a lot of my crap. And Jen didn't. She still doesn't. I've always known that she could pretty much have her choice of men. I didn't think moss would grow under feet when I left—not that she said so; I just sensed it.

I'm still trying to figure out the monogamy stuff. There are two sides to it. If you're deeply in love, the idea of your partner doing the horizontal bop with someone else curls the heart right out of your chest. Also, it's a jungle out there. AIDS, all the STDs—who needs it? It's too risky these days, choosing one from Column A and one from Column B. But I also truly believe that every human being, male or female, is susceptible to that flash that comes when you look across a room and see someone, and suddenly, no matter how long you've been married, no matter how long you've lived with someone, whoever came before that person is void, at least for a while. Maybe parrots hang out together for life, but people? I don't know.

GUY IS A THIRTY-FIVE-YEAR-OLD LAWYER WHO LIVES WITH HIS WIFE, FRAN, IN HOUSTON, TEXAS. THE COUPLE HAS BEEN MARRIED TWELVE YEARS. THEY HAVE THREE CHILDREN.

I really think most guys my age are starved for fun. You get caught in the wife-house-baby routine at too young an age, and before you know it, all the zest is gone. Fran and I got married when I was in my second year of law school; we had our first child two years later. . . . I mean, yes, of course, I was grateful to her—she helped put me through school by working as a secretary—but "grateful" doesn't equal "excitement." After graduation, I was offered this fantastic job in Houston, so we moved down here. But all the other young guys in the firm were single, and they had these great condos with pools, and all these hot-looking women around, while there *I* was, coming home to a ranch house filled with rubber ducks and diapers, plus Fran was pregnant again. It wasn't exactly this swinging lawyer's life.

After we'd been down here about a year, I began seeing Melissa, a lawyer I worked with—casually at first, but she was so much more vivacious than my wife, so much more interested in me, that once we got involved, it started to snowball. She was great in bed—as Marla Maples would say, "the best sex I ever had"—

whereas at home, the whole goddamn bedroom smelled like milk. Fran was breastfeeding the new baby, and it really turned me off. Melissa and I shared so many interests, too—jazz, sailing; when we were together, I forgot about responsibilities. It was wild.

But when Fran found out, it was horrible. She was devastated, and it didn't exactly work in her favor, to let me see all that raw misery. Every time I tried to talk to her, she started crying. Her eyes were all red, her face was swollen . . . she looked like a wreck. And I remember thinking, "No matter what happens, I don't want to spend the rest of my life like this. I will not spend the rest of my life like this.

I was seriously considering divorce—I'd even got the papers going—when out of nowhere, Fran did a total about-face. I still don't know why. Maybe she just got smart. Anyway, she pulled herself together—hired a sitter three afternoons a week so she could go back to school and get her degree; she started fixing herself up again; she stopped letting the kids take over the house. Suddenly, she was looking and acting like the old Fran. I don't know whether it was going back to school or what, but she became more . . . what would you call it?—outer-oriented, I guess. She began reading the newspaper, suggesting we have other couples over for dinner, go out to clubs. Now we had something to talk about besides babies and the broken vacuum cleaner. And she'd slimmed down, had her hair fixed. She'd begun to wear make-up again. Hey, you can say things like that don't matter, but they do. I was proud to be seen around with her. We put the idea of a third child on hold, too. In fact, Alex was born only last year.

It may sound cruel to say this, but I'm trying to be honest. I'm certain that if Fran hadn't changed, I would have left. Call it selfish, call it insensitive, call it whatever you like, but the way I see it, you have only one life to live and that wasn't the way I wanted to spend mine—missing out on everything.

NATHAN IS A FIFTY-TWO-YEAR-OLD SALESMAN FOR A PRINTING COMPANY WHO LIVES WITH HIS GIRLFRIEND, DEE, IN MINNEAPOLIS. THE COUPLE HAS BEEN TOGETHER FIVE YEARS. NATHAN HAS THREE CHILDREN FROM A MARRIAGE THAT ENDED SEVEN YEARS AGO.

When Dee and I first moved in together, we were like two trains constantly overtaking each other. Her train would race ahead; mine would fall back; my train would race ahead; *hers* would fall back . . . like a game of cat and mouse. By that, I mean that our love wasn't consistent—we never seemed to have a time when our feelings were equally intense, when we were each giving our all to the relationship. And maybe because in the beginning, I'd been the one who was most in love, and who had pursued her, I found that very unsettling.

Another problem was that even though right after my divorce I'd fooled around a lot, my head was still back somewhere in the "idyllic" fifties—the whole Donna-Reed–white-picket-fence–dog-in-the-yard routine—and Dee was totally different. Some of her values really bothered me—how careless she was about money; her artsy, flower-child outlook; a spontaneity that often bordered on the insane. "Hey, let's go to Prague," she said out of nowhere, a few months after we'd met. And I'm thinking, Prague? Who goes to Prague? To the lake for a picnic, maybe, or even L.A. for a week when it's twenty below zero here, but *Prague?* So I said, "Uh, uh; not me; no Prague." I was—still am—the kind of a guy who likes to see a Schwarzenegger movie and be in bed by eleven. So right from the start, we had a lot of conflicts going, and after about a year, I began thinking that I was in over my head. I mean, yes, she was exciting; I was wild about her mind. But who needs a mind at midnight, when your hormones are raging? That isn't to say the sex wasn't good—it was. It was just that I was beginning to wonder if I really needed a woman this complicated and off the wall. What I forgot was that "simple" and "sane" hadn't worked out very well when I was married.

Anyway, I began to try and talk myself into believing that Dee wasn't for me. I even made a list of everything about her I didn't like: she smoked; she didn't have a real job—Dee's a freelance illustrator; she had all these crazy friends she kept lending money to. . . . I even convinced myself that she had an alcohol problem. She'd have a couple of glasses of wine at a party, and be talking and laughing, and there I'd be standing to one side, arms crossed in front of me, frowning. I must have been a real joy to live with.

The girl I was seeing on the side abetted all this, of course. Helene kept asking me what kind of life I thought I was going to have with an aging hippie. Besides, she added, everybody knew what artists were like, and on top of it all, the woman was a hopeless drunk, whereas she, Helene, was ready to give me the normal, healthy life-style I deserved. I don't know, she was so aggressive, and I was so confused, that one day I said to Dee, "I'm not getting what I want out of this relationship." She turned to me slowly—I remember, she'd been brushing her hair at the mirror—and put down the bursh and said: "What is it you want that you're not getting, Nathan?" She wasn't being sarcastic; it was as if she really wanted to know. And for some reason, that made me so mad I yelled, "You're supposed to figure that out," and made for the door.

But as soon as I left Dee for Helene, almost the very same day, I started missing her. I kept comparing Helene to her—Dee was so much brighter, funnier, softer. Helene was an organizer, like me; she ran a tight little ship. My shirts were starched; dinner was hot and on time; the apartment was so clean it smelled like a hospital. But I'd look at Helene sometimes and think: "What the hell am I doing here with this strange woman who was probably a Nazi commandant in another life?" And I'd get more and more depressed.

Finally, big man that I was, I decided to call Dee and see how she was doing, although we'd only been separated about three weeks. I mean, how patronizing can you get? But as I saw it, her life was in my hands. I was all set to comfort her, but she sounded as if she was doing just fine, which made me crazy. I felt she should be jumping off bridges, wringing out towels from all the tears. Why wasn't she in mourning, in black for a year? She'd been my property, my turf. I was dying to ask her if she was dating anybody, but she didn't bring it up, and anyway, I kind of didn't want to know the answer.

Then, a few days later, Dee called me at work and said she'd like me to come over that night and pick up the rest of my clothes. When I got there, she was wearing an outfit that was in what I call "mid-slut range"—short-shorts, a skimpy little top, plus, I could see she wasn't wearing any underwear. It wasn't contrived, because she'd often dressed like that when we were together. If it had been, it wouldn't have worked. She didn't come on in a sexual way, either—even sat on the opposite end of the couch—but she just about drove me wild with lust. So the next day I called and we made a date to have dinner in a dumpy little red-checked-tablecloth place we used to go to. After the hospital smell at Helene's, it was a relief to see that one of the wine glasses had spots on it. Dee came in looking terrific, acting very friendly, and sitting that close to her, smelling her, brushing against her, well, I just lost it—suggested we go back to her place and have sex. And she said, "What? You want me to do *what?*" She was a little bit mad, but kind of laughing at the same time. Maybe that's why I went back—sex and laughing. It's an unbeatable combination, and very hard to find.

The other big point is that Dee didn't try to change into something I wanted her to be—or thought I wanted her to be. She stayed who she was, and by doing that, gave me the chance to see that she was what I wanted after all.

MATT IS A FORTY-THREE YEAR-OLD ADVERTISING COPYWRITER. HE LIVES WITH HIS WIFE, GEORGIA, IN ARDSLEY, NEW YORK. THE COUPLE HAS BEEN MARRIED FOURTEEN YEARS. THEY HAVE TWO CHILDREN.

When I met Dana, about a year and a half ago, my whole world was crashing in around me. I'd lost one job and was fighting to keep another. That's often the way the advertising world goes, but on top of it all we were in a recession; agencies were competing like crazy for accounts; men who'd been working at the same place for ten or twenty years would come back from lunch and find out they'd been fired, locked out of their offices. . . . I was, quite frankly, petrified. Georgia and I had always lived above our income, too—we had a four-bedroom house in a pricey suburb, two cars, the kids were into riding lessons; our eldest daughter, Daphne, was getting really good, and her instructor was talking about entering her in some shows. It didn't seem as if there was anything to give up—the lessons, or the cars, or the house. Everything we had seemed vital, you know?

Georgia's job wasn't affected by the economic climate. She's a physical therapist at a big hospital, so she didn't understand why I was so panicked. But every day I was out there, wheeling and dealing and staying up half the night to finish projects so the agency would think I was irreplaceable, so we wouldn't lose the account. Between lack of sleep and worrying every minute, sometimes I felt as if I were on the verge of a breakdown. I was drinking a lot, too—at lunch, after work, on the train. I just wasn't thinking straight. It didn't occur to me at the time that having an affair wasn't going to solve any problems; it was only going to add to them.

Anyway, into this whirlpool walked Dana. She was twenty-nine—fun, easygoing, in retrospect I suppose a little superficial, but maybe that's what I needed. With her, I never had to think. We'd have drinks, and go to movies, or sometimes I'd go up to her place and she'd cook a simple dinner. . . . It was all kind of innocent, but easy. Of course, even I realized it was easy because the real world didn't encroach, but I was sick of the real world—all the hustling and pressure. At home, it was only more of the same—Georgia seemingly unable to understand what I was going through, the girls were at me every minute for ballet lessons or clothes, Daphne even nagged me about getting her own horse. So more and more, I didn't go home till very late at night. Between work and Dana, that wasn't hard to do.

The first night I stayed over at Dana's was because I'd missed the last train. It was all very cozy, very comfortable. And in the morning, when I walked to work—her apartment was only a few blocks from my office—I started thinking "Maybe life doesn't have to be so complicated. Maybe I can start stripping, simplifying." Dana was only temping until she'd saved up enough money to live in Tuscany for a year, and I even began fantasizing about quitting my job and going with her. I still lived at home, but basically I'd already left. I refused to deal with anything unless I absolutely had to—the kids, getting the house painted, getting the pool fixed—anything. And in fact, I couldn't deal with anything. I was totally burned out. So when I finally moved in with Dana, I wasn't thinking about my family, or my future; I wasn't thinking, period. I just knew I had to get out or I'd explode.

Georgia's reaction was cold fury. She immediately started in on what it was going to cost me—that she'd make sure I paid for all this. By the time she and her lawyers got through with me, she said, I wouldn't be able to afford a broom closet, much less the airfare to Tuscany. It was stupid of me to have told her about Tuscany, I know. I don't know why I did that. It just came out. She said she'd call my boss, too—make sure I got fired—which didn't make any sense, considering that she'd already told me she'd be out to get me financially. But at that point she could have threatened me with jail, I was so desperate. I didn't care about anything anymore.

At first, life with Dana was exactly what I needed. She never worried; she had no interest at all in possessions. She was also into positive thinking, crystals—stuff I'd ordinarily have laughed at, but at that point in my life I'd have latched onto anything that seemed like an answer.

It was the certainty that Georgia finally understood what I was going through that made me want to stop looking for easy answers and be a grownup again. As soon as she realized what seriously bad shape I was in, she began really listening. She called me at work and told me how worried she was—insisted on seeing me. We met a few times for drinks, and then she invited me back to the house for dinner. The minute I walked in, I sensed that something had changed—home had gotten an awful lot more quiet, somehow. The kids weren't nagging and complaining, nobody was demanding anything of me—it was nice. Peaceful. Over coffee, after the kids had gone upstairs to do their homework, Georgia told me she knew she'd played a big part in how spoiled they were, but that now she'd made it very clear to them they were lucky to have a father who cared so much, and worked so hard. She also said she loved me no matter what— that if I lost my job, well then, I lost it; *I* was what was important to her. She said that if I'd had an affair, well then, I'd had one but she knew why I'd had one, and life was going to be different now.

If I had to say why I went back in one simple sentence, it would be: "Georgia took the heat off."

JOHN IS A THIRTY-EIGHT-YEAR-OLD PHARMACIST WHO LIVES WITH HIS WIFE, ROSE, IN A SUBURB OF DETROIT. THE COUPLE HAS BEEN MARRIED FIVE YEARS. THEY HAVE NO CHILDREN.

For me, it was purely a sexual thing. In a very basic way, I always loved my wife, but I felt inhibited in bed with her. In my affairs—I had three in the first four years of my marriage—I could be as wild and kinky as I liked, and nobody got hurt . . . or so I thought.

But Rose had really hurt me, too. One time, soon after we were married, I suggested we try oral sex, and she acted as if I was some kind of pervert. The look on her face when she refused was one of open disgust, and that made me feel really bad. I'd asked around a little, and quite a few of the guys I knew told me their wives seemed happy to do it. So I thought the fact that Rose was revolted by the idea had something to do with me personally—that I wasn't attractive enough, or good enough in bed. I'm not the greatest looking; I mean, I'm no Tom Cruise— I'm on the short side, wear glasses—and although Rose had certainly seemed turned on when we started dating, I now began to wonder why she'd married me in the first place—just because I made a good salary? For the life-style? Rose comes from a big, blue-collar, Catholic family, and she'd always said she'd never live that way, with kids running around all over the place, and not enough money. I could understand that, but it was pretty painful to think maybe she'd married me for security, that she didn't really love me at all.

Neither of us had had much sexual experience before we got married, but I'd always believed that was a big reason people did get married, to have a great sex life. I was all set to try new techniques, but whenever I brought anything up, anything that deviated from the missionary position—during which, by the way, she lay there practically gritting her teeth—forget it. Take the night I brought home this book on how to make your sex life better; it was as much for her as it was for me. I left it on the bureau in the bedroom, and the minute she saw it, she picked it up with two fingers and tossed it in the garbage—said she wouldn't have filth like that in the house. Look, I'm making her sound like a witch, and she wasn't . . . isn't. It was just in this one area that our signals were crossed. But anyway, that was the night I gave up on the idea of great sex within marriage, and started looking for someone to fool around with. It was what I figured I had to do to get along.

It wasn't that hard to find someone—much easier, in fact, than it had been when I was single. There was Sally, and then Tracey, and then Laurie. Laurie was the one Rose found out about. She was absolutely beside herself—demanded that I end it—and I got so mad I moved into Laurie's apartment for a few months. Who the hell was she to tell me what to do, this wife who just lay there like she was doing me a favor every time I got her to agree to have sex? But then Laurie started pressuring me to leave Rose, and Rose was on the phone all the time, telling me she'd never give me a divorce; she was going to fight it all the way. At one point she even threatened to sue for half my practice, and that really turned me off. It made me actively want to leave her. Her family got in on it, too—everybody advising her and telling her what her rights were. It was quite a scene. Nobody seemed to understand that I'd never wanted a divorce. I just wanted some of the sex I wasn't getting at home.

What made me go home was that Rose did a total turn-around—stopped yelling and threatening, and really seemed to want to listen to me. At first, I was nervous about opening up, but I explained how her rejection had made me feel. And she explained some, too—told me that the way she'd grown up had caused her to have some pretty rigid ideas about sex. She also said that at times, I'd seemed so focused on sex, she'd felt that was all I wanted—not her, as a person.

We may wind up seeing a sex therapist, but right now, we're really trying to make it work on our own. Rose, particularly, is making a big effort—asks me what I want her to do, and all that. And I'm being careful about not overwhelming her. Now that she'll let me show her a few things, without pushing me away, I'm starting to feel like a desirable man again. It's quite a turn-on playing teacher.

ROB IS A FORTY-FIVE-YEAR-OLD INVESTMENT BANKER WHO LIVES WITH HIS SECOND WIFE, JOAN, IN NEW YORK CITY AND SOUTHAMPTON, LONG ISLAND. THE COUPLE HAS BEEN MARRIED TWELVE YEARS. EACH HAS ONE CHILD FROM A PREVIOUS MARRIAGE.

I never thought of myself as the kind of man who'd fool around. My first marriage was a disaster—we were both children, really—and when it ended after only ten months, I had six years of bachelorhood in New York. It was a wonderful time for me. I was earning a lot, girls were everywhere, sex was everywhere. So, when I met Joan, I felt I'd sown my oats and was ready for a grownup life.

I guess the problem was that it got to be too "grownup." Joan had been so sexy and spontaneous, but she started really getting into the social bit in Southampton on weekends—we have a country house there—and after a while we ended up talking more about who was going to sit next to whom at our Saturday night dinner party than who was going to be on top in bed. The other thing was that I began to get the feeling she was competing with me all the time. I had plenty of that at the office, and the last thing I needed when I came home at night was to have more of the same.

Anyway, it was getting awfully tense at home, so when this gorgeous thirty-year-old single decorator—her name was Gail—started coming on to me at a cocktail party one night, I couldn't resist. I called to ask her out for lunch the next day, and exactly one week later we were in bed together.

This went on for about six months—you know, nooners, fake business trips, "working late" to close a deal. But finally, I just couldn't stand the duplicity anymore, so I told Joan. She was very bitter, very sarcastic. "A decorator?" she said. "That's really hilarious. I hope she has your new apartment decorated for you, because you're certainly not staying here." I hadn't really thought about physically leaving home until then, but that did it. I packed my bags, called Gail, and within twenty minutes, I was at her place.

And for a while, it was great. Long, romantic evenings in expensive restaurants with this woman who was really interested in me; sex the way I'd forgotten it could be; movies, long walks; carriage rides through the park—all the things Joan and I had stopped doing years before. I was flying.

Amazingly, after her initial outburst, Joan was terrific. Whenever I saw her, she was always very civilized, very cool. Our friends weren't so great, though. Most of them, including my college roommate and his wife, decided that I was a real heel and dropped me altogether.

Then there was Gail, who kept pressuring me to get on with the divorce. She was young, and wanted her own family, and one day—I'll never forget it—I was sitting at my desk just about to go out to lunch with a major client, and I suddenly saw that I was heading straight into something that probably wouldn't be half as good as what I'd left. Not to be crass about it, but I realized that if I wanted to maintain my current life-style, I'd be pretty strapped, trying to support a whole new family plus an ex-wife and a son almost ready for college. I didn't like the way Gail was nagging me, either. Her personality seemed to have changed a lot since we'd met. So I did a weird thing. Right after lunch, I called Joan and asked if I could come up to the apartment. She said "of course"—she was always so nice to me now—and the minute she opened the door I knew I wanted to come home.

It was pretty tough at the beginning. Gail was totally destroyed—she'd lost her job, even had a mini-breakdown and had to spend a few weeks in the hospital—so there I was, feeling guilty about her and wanting to make things work with Joan, not even sure of what I was doing half the time. Then Gail got better, Joan and I started seeing a marriage counselor, and now we're back on pretty solid ground. She doesn't try to outdo me at everything anymore, and she's sexy again—she likes to sleep with me, and lets me know it.

If I have any advice to give a woman whose husband has left

her, it would be to do three things: be patient, be strong, and probably most important of all, forgive him. Joan seemed to forgive me right away. She'd done a lot of thinking while I was gone, and I guess she realized she really wanted this marriage, and that to punish me if and when I came back would only destroy any chance we had of making things good again.

In my experience, most men like a little outside fun once in a while. They love the thrill of the chase, but deep down, they don't really want to walk away from their home, their family, their roots. I think that if more women could manage to be as calm and understanding as Joan was, more men would come back.

LARRY IS A FIFTY-TWO-YEAR-OLD PROFESSOR WHO LIVES WITH HIS WIFE, DIANE, IN LOS ANGELES. THE COUPLE HAS BEEN MARRIED TWENTY-ONE YEARS. THEY HAVE A GROWN DAUGHTER.

My wife just isn't a very warm person. In a way, it's not her fault—she grew up in a home where nobody ever kissed or patted or hugged, and oh, sure, I always knew she loved me, but whenever I tried to hold her hand, or put my arm around her, she'd pull away. And she almost never touched me, either—in bed, out of bed, anywhere. Sometimes I wanted affection so badly I thought I was going to die. That sounds dramatic, but it really was that bad. And I finally realized that I'd have to go somewhere else to get it, not just in bed but to help me through the day.

I met a young associate physics instructor one summer when I was at a conference in Boulder, and she was so . . . physical is the word, I guess, so open and loving and tender. I fell head over heels in love. It's over three years now, and I can still remember how I felt.

I helped Nina get a job in L.A. so she could be near me, and we were together four and a half years. I never actually left my wife, but I was at Nina's apartment a lot, and sometimes spent the night. Sex wasn't the big thing, though. It was the affection. My wife knew what was going on, of course—she's far from stupid—but she didn't seem to mind. Or at least, that's what I thought. I thought she was probably glad I was having an affair; that way, she didn't have to bother with me except as someone who'd take her to parties or sit across the dinner table from her. It seemed to me that all she was concerned with was appearances, and having a husband was part of that front. I felt that if she'd cared for me at all, she would have put up a fight. But she didn't, and life went on pretty much as it always had.

Then one day, I came home from Nina's early and found Diane rocking back and forth, holding my picture, tears streaming down her face. She tried to turn away so that I couldn't see, but I went over to her and put my arms around her, and this time, she let me. And it was then I knew that I had to stop what I was doing. I suddenly realized it wasn't that Diane didn't have any emotions, she just couldn't express them. And I hadn't done much to help her; I'd simply gone to someone else for what I wasn't getting. Even now, the thought of her sitting there with that picture breaks my heart.

Since then, I've made a big effort to be more understanding, and now that Diane knows how I feel, she's trying hard, too. She'll never be as warm and open and physical as Nina, but she's better.

I don't want this to sound as if I went back to Diane because I felt sorry for her. It's a lot more complex than that. I went back because, maybe for the first time, I realized how much she loved me. And when I knew that, I knew there was hope.

It's funny, but sometimes I think having Nina around all those years kept me married.

JAMES IS A FIFTY-NINE-YEAR-OLD ENGINEER WHO LIVES WITH HIS WIFE, NADINE, IN BALTIMORE. THE COUPLE HAS BEEN MARRIED THIRTY-FIVE YEARS. THEY HAVE FOUR CHILDREN.

All this happened over twelve years ago, and I still can't quite believe I did what I did. I jeopardized my marriage, career, children, and all for someone I not only didn't love, I didn't even like. Not a single friend could understand what I saw in Tricia. She was cold and calculating and not very bright—some ten years younger than my wife, yes, but I don't think that was it. Nadine is much more attractive. She also more loving, sweeter, nicer. Believe me, I've thought and thought and I've never been able to figure it out. But for over a year, I was obsessed with Tricia. When she told me she was pregnant, I immediately set her up in an apartment, and then left Nadine and moved in with her. It was as if I'd been waiting for a reason to leave. But even when I found out that Tricia had lied—she hadn't been pregnant at all—it didn't change my feelings. I couldn't wait to leave work and be with her.

I don't know how Nadine was able to keep on loving me throughout the affair, but she did; her love never faltered. Even when I told her I was leaving, there were no recriminations, no threats. Her eyes just got very bright, and her lips were trembling, but all she said was, "If you feel you must, James, then I guess you must. There is nothing I could say or do that would keep you here, feeling the way you do."

Looking back, you could hardly say she gave up on me though. She called almost every day to see how I was, kept me filled in on the children, who, of course were well on their way to hating me by then. But she never tried to turn them against me—in fact, it was just the opposite—she made sure I saw them often. Once, when I was in the hospital in traction for ten days—an old back problem had acted up—she checked to see if Tricia was going to visit that night (She wasn't, naturally; she came exactly twice, and stayed ten minutes each time.) So Nadine brought over a favorite meal of mine she'd cooked. I can still remember how good that lasagna tasted. She even smuggled in a bottle of wine. All this might make her seem like a fool, the sort of woman you could walk all over, but honestly, it wasn't weakness. It was more like strength. When the affair began, we'd been married twenty-three years, and I think Nadine felt there was too much between us, too much history, too much love, to simply throw away. In her head, no matter what, she was my wife, and instant divorce was not an option. She didn't get angry when she refused to give me one—just quietly told me she still loved me, would always love me and that I owed it to her and the kids to wait at least a year before I made any drastic moves, because this wasn't love, it was obsession. And it would destroy all our lives if I gave in to it.

Now that I'm back home, I still shudder when I think of what would have happened if I *had* given in to it. Now, it all seems like a nightmare—a terrible, terrible dream.

CHAPTER 11

Now That

He's Back...

What Next?

"I can't believe it. I'm so deliriously happy, I feel like a totally different person," says Liza, a forty-one-year-old production editor. "Tony has only been back for three days, and it's better than it's ever been, in all of our sixteen years together. He calls from his office to see if everything's okay with me, writes little love notes and leaves them on my pillow in the morning, suggests we meet for drinks after work. Drinks after work! We haven't done that since we were first dating; it almost feels decadent. He's turned into a dream husband, and I have to pinch myself occasionally to be sure it's really happening."

But then her face clouds, and she adds softly, "Do you know what scares me, though? Me. I still have so much pent-up rage at Tony for having dared to fool around that sometimes, right in the midst of all this wonderfulness, I have an overwhelming urge to start screaming, to slap him, rake my nails down his cheeks. I sit tight on my anger, but I'm secretly terrified it's going to get the better of me someday. I love Tony, and I desperately want the reconciliation to work. But I've been through so much, I'm having a hard time acting as if the affair never happened. He put me through hell, and I just can't forget it."

Like Liza, you won't be able to forget the affair happened, either—and you shouldn't. Repressing the truth, and your feelings about it, will only make you even angrier. But control those feelings you must, if you're to give your relationship the second chance it deserves. During all the preceding steps, you may have played the game like a total pro, but what you have to guard against now are the lengths to which wounded pride, rage, and mistrust may take you. Yes, this is your big opportunity to have him forever, but it's a tricky time because, underneath, you're not truly over what happened. During your attempt to get him back, you've been sitting on a lot of powerful emotions, and now that you actually have him, it's perfectly normal to feel you might explode at any moment. It's one thing to rationalize about a husband or lover having an affair, and quite another to have the body that had the affair lying next to you in bed night after night. No matter how much you tell yourself the idea of the other woman as supersiren is a myth, you can't help wondering if *your* man's other woman might have been the exception. And as you may already have found out, none of this is exactly conducive to glorious lovemaking.

What's more, you *are* hurt, you *are* furious—what woman in her right mind wouldn't be? But remember how strong and focused you've been through all this? Well, you're going to have to keep calling on that strength. Now is not the time to cave in—to indulge the almost uncontrollable urge to get even. What you absolutely cannot do is allow old negative emotions to destroy this chance for a new beginning. If you phone his office constantly to check up on him, question him every time he's five minutes late, all the valiant efforts you've made so far will have been for nothing. You may need extra therapy at this stage to help you understand and control your feelings—many women do. You might even try therapy together—if he's willing. Don't push it if he's not, though; you can do a lot on your own, with the help of a good counselor.

You'll also want to steer clear of the sort of "friends" who are only too happy to undermine your venture. ("You took him back after what he did to you? Where's your self-respect? If *my* husband had an affair, I'd never even speak to him again.") Friends like this you don't need, especially not right now. They'll just fuel your anger, make you come across—sorry, we've got to say it—as annoyingly self-righteous.

The point is, like it or not, affairs happen; it's how you *handle* them that makes the difference. As family therapist Sandra Finzi noted in an article in the May-June 1989 issue of *Family Therapy Networker*, the attitude toward straying is very different in Europe—and is something at least to think about. "Rather than viewing infidelities as an indication of a deep character flaw," Finzi said, "most Europeans are far more relaxed with the idea that acting on sexual longing depends more on availability of opportunity than the state of one's marriage or the condition of one's psyche. It was this attitude that Mozart immortalized when he wrote his great opera *Così Fan Tutte* ("So Does Everyone")."

Now, if you're a typical American woman, you won't be able to be quite so devil-may-care about your man's infidelity. We bring up the *Così Fan Tutte* approach only because it's worth remembering that many other cultures are more accepting of humanity's frailties, and that women living in them are therefore much less likely to allow the rage, jealousy, or desire for revenge that typically surface during an affair's aftermath to poison their primary relationships. Like us, they think fidelity is a swell idea; *un*like us, they tend not to do a "never darken my door again" number if their man strays. The ladies are just a touch more realistic about human sexual nature.

Don't forget, too, that your man has indicated he's ready to redefine both you and the relationship; he's agreed to new terms; he's reaffirmed his love; he has, in many crucial ways, changed. And so have you. Naturally, you wish the affair had never happened, but what might have been (or not been) no longer matters.

You are both here, now, at a vital crossroads. Love, trust, consideration, and honest communication must be the cornerstones of your new relationship. Give him the best of the new you, and you'll get the best of the new him back.

To give your man the best of the woman you now are, you have to forgive him—if you don't, there's no way the relationship can flourish. Just saying the words isn't enough, either; you have to really mean it. Otherwise, the hurt and anger will always be there, waiting, just beneath the surface, and will prevent you from loving fully, richly, in the way you want to love.

"The wish to hurt, to retaliate, to be proved right, even to extract a confession of wrongdoing from a mate is normal," say Drs. Connell Cowan and Melvyn Kinder. "But ultimately when the anger begins to cool, the final step in restoring love and harmony is forgiveness. Forgiving unblocks love. No matter how hurt or angry you are, irrespective of how right you may feel, and regardless of how much you may blame or want to strike back, you can't love again in a positive way until you choose to forgive."

Why can't you truly love again unless you forgive? Well, for one thing, leftover pain and anger will still be churning around in there somewhere, coloring your every move with your man—and that doesn't make for a warm, trusting relationship. Simply denying that you ever were hurt or mad doesn't work, either. Instead, you have to say to yourself, "Yes, he caused me a lot of grief; yes, I still hurt," and then consciously let go of such feelings.

Forgiveness is a whole lot easier if you start seeing your man as he actually is—not as some paragon of malehood you've cooked up in your head, but as a fallible, vulnerable human being with strengths and weaknesses all his own. When you do, you won't confuse him with fantasy (doomed, because he'll never be able to live up to it) and will then be able to love and accept him, "not as your savior but as another wounded human being, struggling to be healed," as therapist Harville Hendrix put it in *Getting The Love You Want*.

Hendrix believes that on a subconscious level, all marriages or in-depth relationships are about healing childhood wounds, and when a couple realizes that all-important fact, the two will understand their union better, have more control over it. If you fly into a rage when your man fails to notice you've just had your hair cut, for example, you may be reacting to long-buried, hurtful memories of the times your mother withheld approval when you were little. But is it fair to take it out on him because Mom ignored your A-studded report card or never showed up for intramural soccer? Yes, he had an affair and that hurt, but you can't blame the man for every single life blow from age two on up. (Nor should he blame you because his older sister was a sadist who called him a sissy and locked him in the closet.) Knowing who it is you're really mad at minimizes clashes, and helps make your relationship the supportive, restorative union you both need. He's wounded, you're wounded—the idea is to understand that and help each other out, not cause more hurt.

Hendrix adds that to create a healthy, nurturing relationship, you must "learn to value your partner's needs and wishes as highly as you value your own." How true that is, and how often we sabotage ourselves with "where's mine?" kind of thinking. Hendrix doesn't say *more* highly, notice; he says *as* highly. Throughout this book, we've been hammering away at putting yourself first. Now, however, your man's back, and his wants matter, too. We're not for a second suggesting that you "sacrifice" yourself, or let yourself be used. But one of the very best ways to get what *you* need is to give him what *he* needs. Sensitivity to those needs (he should be sensitive to yours, too, of course; we hope that goes without saying) is critical if reconciliation is to succeed.

"It was weird at first," says Barrie, a twenty-nine-year-old high-school French teacher who got back together with her husband, Grant, after a year-long separation.

> Our patterns of relating had become so ingrained that neither of us even realized they were there. It had mostly to do with little things—he'd always expect me to clear the table after dinner, for instance, even though I'd worked

just as hard as he had; I always expected him to mow the lawn—after all, he was the man! Well, one night, after he'd been home for about two weeks, I was loading the dishwasher, and I just exploded. Then, after I was through with my poor-little-me-I-have-to-come-home-after-work-and-play-housewife number, he started in—told me he was fed up with having to do all the "husband" stuff, like the lawn, and taking the car in to have the oil changed, and putting up storm windows. By the time it was over, we were both screaming, but when I calmed down, I realized, for the first time, what I'd been doing. My Dad had had a drinking problem, and had never done anything around the house, so I'd tried to make Grant into this pillar of a husband, one who'd take on all the traditionally male chores. It had nothing to do with what was best for Grant; it was more about my trying to get what I hadn't gotten from my father.

We talked everything out, and Grant said he wouldn't mind helping with the dishes a bit; he'd just never thought I wanted him to, since I seemed so efficient. His mother, he added, had always made a big thing of never letting anyone in the kitchen; she'd yell at Grant and the other kids if they even carried in a plate—grab it out of their hands because they were sure to put it in the dishwasher "wrong." And I said I could easily take the car in sometimes. It was the best talk we'd ever had. Oh, and by the way, we decided to hire someone to mow the lawn!

I think it was great that all this happened so soon after Grant came back, because we were both slipping into old routines, along with all the old grudges and frustrations. Now, we're starting to be more considerate of each other, to really talk, and it's made an enormous difference. I realize he's not my alcoholic father, he realizes I'm not his domineering mother, and we're getting along better now than we ever did. Putting Grant's needs right up there alongside my own has changed everything. It's so simple—I'm surprised more people don't figure it out. And I'm sure our chances of staying together have gone up by about five hundred percent.

Giving his needs as much importance as yours should be at the top of your priority list now that he's back. Here, other insights that will help make this crucial transition smooth, exciting, rewarding.

REMEMBER THAT YOU ARE BOTH DIFFERENT PEOPLE NOW

Yes, you still have the same bodies (unless you've managed to spruce yours up some), same backgrounds, same basic personality traits, but as we've said, what you've been through has changed you both. So look at your man with a fresh perspective. You can't pretend that nothing happened, for a profound bond of trust was broken, but you can learn to appreciate—and respect— the new, more open, honest, caring husband or lover who has emerged from the chaos.

SEE HIM AS A PARTNER, NOT A SAVIOR

Not casting your husband or lover in such a role is vital, according to Harville Hendrix. You have to understand that he needs *you* just as much as you need him. He needs your support, love, compassion—for he's hurting, too. No, he's not perfect (neither are you), nor should you expect him to be. You now know that you can get along without him, and that's good, because it helps take the heat off. You're strong, competent—a survivor—and it's imperative that you keep this image of yourself in mind. Of course, it's better with him, just as it's better for him with you, but he's only a part of what you need to be happy. When you see this clearly, you won't live in terror that he'll take off again the minute you displease him (saviors need a lot of servicing; at least, that's how you see it), or put him in the position of having to fulfill your every need. Rather, you'll operate as an equal, which is a lot more fun for you both.

"I was so nervous when Chris moved back, I started acting like my old, insecure self again," Sue recalls.

> I was afraid he wouldn't like what I cooked for dinner, or that he might think the house had gotten sort of rundown while he was gone, or that he'd be mad I'd gotten a puppy during his absence. But then I woke up on morning and thought, "Hey, wait a minute; you're that same woman who can live by herself and have a pretty good time doing it. Chris is wonderful, but he doesn't define you. So enough of this nonsense." And right after that, everything began to get better. I'm more relaxed, more confident than I've ever been with Chris, and he loves it—seems delighted by how spunky and self-assured I've become. We're on a more equal footing now, and it's great. Just yesterday, he told me how terrific it was not to feel that if he made one wrong move, I'd start crying, or feel he didn't love me. Having to be everything to me must have been a pretty heavy burden.

I LOVE HIM FOR WHO HE REALLY IS

Chip away at the illusions and look at the flesh-and-blood man—no more of that if-only-he-made-more-money, or if-only-he-were-six-inches-taller-and-had-a-thirty-four-inch-waist stuff. Nobody likes to spend time around someone who feels they don't measure up. You can bet that if you have these negative feelings about him, you're communicating them, if only on a subconscious level. So stand back, and take a careful look at who he is—at all those qualities you fell in love with in the first place. His natural sweetness, curiosity, wit, perhaps. His intelligence, sensitivity. Focus on his strengths; review them every single morning.

Before long, you'll actually begin to see him differently—more realistically and positively—and you can be sure he'll pick up on your new attitude and respond. Approval is infectious; he'll start to appreciate you in new ways, too, and soon, great chunks of tension will fall away because you two are just being who you are.

Anne-Marie, whose husband never actually moved out, but was involved with another woman for six months, had this to say:

> It embarrasses me even to admit it, but I used to be pretty hard on Stan. I was always saying things like, "You know, if you worked a little harder we might be able to afford to join the country club like Alice and Mark." or "I guess you heard that George gave Debbie a gorgeous silver fox coat for Christmas," or, even worse, "I probably should have married Keith Mitchell; he's the president of his own ad agency now." No wonder Stan wanted to run. And if the girlfriend did anything for us—for me—she helped me realize what a treasure Stan was, and what a bitch I'd been for so long. He's such a dear, loving person, and it's ironic that it took something like another woman in his life to force me to wake up to what I'd had all along.

REALIZE HE'S NOT A MIND READER

Often, when we're close to someone, we expect that person to know exactly what we need, without any input on our part. Well, guess what? It doesn't work this way. "As much as we might desire it, a mate is never a mind reader," say Cowan and Kinder. "We cannot assume that a mate always knows our wishes, hopes, and hurts. Ultimately, we are responsible for making ourselves known to those we love."

"Oh, but when we first fell in love, all he had to do was look at me and he knew," you may be thinking. And indeed, that could well be the case—lots of starry-eyed young couples are so wrapped up in each other that a blink or a sigh is enough to conjure up immediate awareness. But if you think about it, you'll see that an intensity that fierce wouldn't be healthy over the long term—you'd shut out the rest of the world! Beside, it's expecting an awful lot of a partner to operate as a live-in telepathist— especially when he's trying to figure out how to pay the mortgage.

Face it, then, unless he's one in a hundred million, your man is simply not going to turn into the Amazing Kreskin. (You probably wouldn't want him to, anyway, considering some of the things that are going on in your mind at present.) So sitting around pouting—or storming around, yelling—because he doesn't pick up on the fact that you're exhausted and would like to be taken out to dinner is ridiculous. On days when you haven't the strength to lift a cup, much less cook, call him and tell him so. The same goes for the more intimate parts of your relationship. Not interested in sex right now, but could sure use a hug? Let the man in on your secret! Feel you're going to have a breakdown if his Mom visits for more than a week? Get the message across! He may not agree with everything you say (or be willing to do everything you ask), but lines of communication will be open, and the two of you can then figure out what works for both of you. Sulking is not only a waste of time, it's destructive. How would you like it if he didn't mention that he was dying to watch *Road Warrior* on TV and instead told you yes, fine, go ahead and invite the Murrays over for drinks—then glared at you all evening? Clearly, this saying-what-you-want business works both ways; it's important for him to feel comfortable about telling you what he needs, too. The only way to keep resentments from building up is to talk.

"The day I realized I was acting like a little kid, expecting Gerald simply to know I wasn't feeling well, was the day our marriage changed," says Maria, a forty-eight-year-old copywriter with an L.A. ad agency.

> I was all set to start accusing him of being a selfish, insensitive creep because he hadn't tucked me into bed with hot tea and sympathy, and then I thought, "Hold it; I'm not even sniffling. How is he suppose to figure out I think I'm

coming down with the flu?" So much of my behavior had been childish, and I really didn't like myself that way. So now, when I have a sore throat or PMS, or just wish he'd put down the newspaper and talk to me, whatever it is, I tell him—not like a whiny first-grader, but like a woman. Gerald's better at telling me things, too. Sometimes, when he's not in the mood for sex, for instance, he explains he's really tired; it's not that he doesn't still think I'm the foxiest thing that ever walked down the street. So now when it happens, I don't feel depressed and rejected; I just realize that he's been working too hard and something has to give. Besides, tomorrow's another day, as Scarlett so eloquently put it.

GROW SOME MORE

Remember those great strides you made while he was temporarily out of your life—how you dieted away twelve pounds in eight weeks, signed up for step-aerobics, got back into sculpting at the Thursday night class, trained to become a literacy volunteer and taught a fifty-two-year-old man how to read? Now is no time to slack off. All those accomplishments show—look great on you—and are part of the reason your man returned home. Just because he's back, and the relationship has stabilized—or is in the process of restabilizing—is no reason to slide back into those old self-defeating patterns. You love the person you've become, and must make sure that you continue to nurture new-found parts of yourself. Keep up the step-aerobics, join an even more advanced sculpture class, teach a sixty-two-year-old man to read—and don't be shy about starting other new projects. The busier you are, the happier you'll be; the better you feel about yourself, the better he'll feel about you. Of course, you'll want to leave plenty of time for him and your blossoming new relationship, but remember, you've fought hard to get where you are, and deserve to stay there—mentally and physically.

"The first few weeks Jake was back, I could hardly think of anything except our being together," says a forty-three-year-old bank loan officer.

> I'd rush home and fix an elaborate dinner, we'd sip vintage Bordeaux by candlelight, then fall into each other's arms in bed. As you can imagine, after a few weeks of this bacchanalian life-style, my formerly firm thighs were beginning to jiggle, my skirts were getting tight, and I was more than a little disgusted with myself. Jake never said anything—he probably never even noticed, since we spent most of our time in the dark—but I knew that if I didn't get a grip on my weight right away, it would be a big mistake. Before he had left, I'd really let myself go, and I was absolutely determined never to let that happen again. So I started preparing more sensible meals, and made myself get up every morning and walk two miles before leaving for work. I look and feel so much better now, and also don't have the uneasy feeling that I'm hiding out, which I sometimes did when Jake first moved back in. I adore the man, but I also have a life.

THINK BEFORE YOU ACT

This is just another way to help interrupt some of those old negative patterns before they get too entrenched. Say your man settles down on the sofa to watch Sunday afternoon football. . . . and *you* see red. Before you shriek, "My God, can't you ever get through a weekend without turning that damn thing on?" stop youself and count to eleven. Yes, you think football is barbaric (also, that watching TV hour after hour is totally brain-deadening), but *he* probably views it as a prime source of relaxation, as well as a subliminal way of bonding with the boys in the office. So try to understand how destructive your trashing his pleasure can be. You're not required to love football, or learn the names of all the starting quarterbacks in the Big Ten, but do consider better ways of dealing than yelling or pouting. How about a little discussion at half time, centering on how left out you feel? Then ask if you two couldn't come up with a compromise—one that would let him work in some of the game and let *you* work in some fun and companionship. Whatever you decide on will be better than the stand-off you'd have forced if you'd simply teed off. Too often, we let knee-jerk reactions control us instead of controlling them. It takes practice, but learning to think before you act can do as much to bolster a relationship as anything we've discussed.

ACCEPT YOUR FAULTS

Never an easy thing to do, but therapist Harville Hendrix believes—and we do, too—that by accepting your own limitations you "lessen your tendency to project your negative traits onto your mate, which creates a less hostile environment." We're not suggesting you dwell on qualities you don't like about yourself, simply that you don't deny them. By accepting the rich, complex woman—faults and all—that you are, you'll be able to get along with yourself and others much more effectively. As we've already said, nobody's perfect, you included, and those "bad" qualities are probably not really so bad. Taking responsibility for yourself, the not-so-good as well as the good, not only makes you more likable and easier to be around but it also allows you to have real input in a relationship. You won't always be right (who could be?), but you'll operate as a whole person, complete with the power that entails. If you put yourself on a pedestal you abdicate that power, plus, since you're untouchable, you're going to have to blame someone else whenever something goes wrong. And most often that "someone" is your husband or lover.

"For years, I felt that everything wrong with our marriage was because of Roger," says a fifty-five-year-old pharmacologist.

I thought our sex life was unfulfilling because he was cold. I thought our oldest daughter was having trouble in school because Roger was home so little. I thought he wasn't making more money because he wasn't trying. It was only after therapy that I began to see I'd been blaming him for many of my own problems . . . I hadn't exactly been a sex object myself; I'd always found Lorie hard to deal with, even when she was a little girl. Gradually, I began to accept my role in the bad times our marriage was going through. I even got to the point where I could forgive Roger's involvement with another woman, because I realized he hadn't been getting enough of what he needed from me. It's hard for me to say these things, but they're true. I was far from an ideal wife, and knowing that has made a big difference in the way we relate to each other.

ACCEPT HIS FAULTS, TOO

This doesn't mean you're going to love his refusing to leave his clothes anywhere but on the bedroom chair, or that he's never once in his life been able to figure out how to feed the cat. But you'll have to adjust to these and other foibles if you two are going to have a new and more loving relationship. Faults of the more serious variety—such as a drinking problem or abusive behavior—are obviously something else again. The distinction here is between conduct that requires some adjustment on your part and the sort that's unacceptable by any standard. If his behavior falls into the latter category, confront him, and let him know you simply cannot live with it—not because you don't love him, but because you find what he's doing both threatening and painful. You'd hoped he'd changed during his absence—in fact, he'd swore that he had—but if he doesn't shape up fast, you have no choice but to take action yourself, even if this means putting the relationship on hold until you're certain he's reformed.

What we're mainly talking about, though, are those niggling

little habits that have always made you crazy—like his leaving the toilet seat up, chewing with his mouth open, pulling away from a stoplight so fast the tires screech in protest. Begin by trying to figure out exactly what it is about the behavior that upsets you. If you just think it's rude, or inconsiderate, or upsetting to others, then mention this to him—ever-so-gently, of course. He may not even have been aware of what he was doing. If, on the other hand, his chewing bothers you because your tony, old-money Daddy never chewed that way, or because you're having husband-as-prince fantasies, think again. This man is *not* your father, and you are *not* a little girl. Nor are you exactly Princess Stephanie of Monaco. So try to be a touch more tolerant. You love the darling, right?

PUT THE PAST IN THE PAST

We know how hard this is, but it's really the only way to go. Recriminations, accusations, or punishments will get you nowhere; they'll put strains on your new, still-fragile relationship that may cause it to become unglued. Of course, you may find yourself thinking of *her* at the most inopportune moments— when you hear him whistling in the shower, or when he gives you that sweet little goodbye kiss in the morning—but all this is perfectly natural. What should you do at such times? Well, remember the old *Stop/Switch* trick? Use it now. Whenever you find your mind wandering off to consider what kind of lingerie his girlfriend wore or what they did in bed, just tell your mind to *Stop* and *Switch* to thoughts of the present: How much you adore your man, how to make the union work.

Keep reminding yourself that he choose *you*. Whatever happened, happened. Whatever he did, he did. Whatever you did, you did. But that was then and this is now, and it's now that counts—and tomorrow, and the day after tomorrow. That's where your attention belongs. Make plans, do new things together, keep lines of communication open, and most of all, keep forgiving, laughing, loving.

If all this forgiving sounds next to impossible, it shouldn't, because it isn't. It worked for the couples we talked to, and it can work for you. When you stop trying to protect yourself, or to get even, and start plugging into those tender feelings you've had tucked down inside all along, you'll be well on your way to creating the best, most gratifying relationship you've ever had.

CHAPTER 12

How To

Make It

Better For Both

For Good

He's back. The second honeymoon is over. He's settled in, and much of your life has returned to normal. You've covered a lot of territory in agreeing to put your lives back together, and in many ways, your relationship is stronger than ever. But what now? What's the secret to happily ever after? Well, there are many such secrets, but the most important one, we think, is to love *yourself*—always, totally, no matter what. Sounds like psychobabble maybe, but it's absolutely true. The reason you two have started over is because *you* wanted it that way. You held yourself together—though it was far from easy—made new friends, developed new interests, took care of yourself in dozens of healthy, loving ways, and you must never lose sight of your uniqueness, specialness, the enormous value of just being you.

Keep reminding yourself that

you are a new, stronger, more self-reliant woman. Don't forget that for even one tiny second. *You are the best thing you've got.* He's right up there, and, of course, you're more secure and happy with him than without him, but on your own, you are sturdy, loving, competent, and full of life; the more you're aware of that fact, the better your relationship will be. Remember, too, that when you're feeling content and sure of yourself, you're much less likely to lash out at those close to you. Your man is part of your happiness, but he is not responsible for it. He's not Daddy or Mommy; he's your partner. As you already know, you can't control him; you can only control yourself. If you put yourself first,—not selfishly but lovingly,—you'll be a far better mate, and a far happier woman.

Feeling fine about yourself isn't always easy, because some of those old insecurities are still lurking about. Everybody has them, although there will be days when you feel it's only you who ever feels shaky. But whenever you sense you're starting to slip back into deadly "poor-me," or "I'm nothing" patterns, just call up the *Stop/Switch* technique again. Tempted to flash back to those miserable nights you spent without him, or, even worse, to thoughts of him with her? Say *Stop*, then *Switch* to planning which movie you'd like to see on Saturday night. You can control negative thoughts, and, in fact, you must. Absolutely no good will come of dwelling on the pain of the past. Don't do that to yourself. You've been through enough. This is the time to let go of oppressive baggage and get on with it. You can be happy, you will be happy, you are happy with this man, so enjoy what you've got—and help him enjoy it, too.

In *The Art of Loving*, Erich Fromm says love is "the active concern for the life and growth of that which we love." When you are comfortable with your love for him, and are truly concerned with his "life and growth," he'll feel it, and flourish. You'll be the woman whose love and support keep him charged up and thriving, and he'll adore you for it. As we've said before, if you're the woman who helps him feel good about himself, why would he ever want anyone else?

Here are some other points to keep in mind when it comes to long-term success in your relationship:

REMEMBER THAT LOVE NEVER PUNISHES

Tough as it is to control that urge to strike out when you've been hurt, it's absolutely vital to try. Chances are, you're going to be hypersensitive to little slights—real or imagined—for a while; things that might never have bothered you before now become momentous. He says he'll call around four about dinner plans, and then doesn't, which makes you furious. Who does he think he is? Why does he treat you this way? How can he do this to you? Nonsense! The odds are heavy he's not doing anything to you. It's probably that something came up, and he simply forgot. It doesn't do any good to personalize such actions, and you certainly don't want to get into a punishment mode. As much as you can, try to see things from *his* point of view—and always remember that this is *the man you love*. He's human; he's fallible; he makes mistakes. And you do, too. The acceptance of this fallibility on both your parts is what the give and take of marriage is all about.

CONFRONT YOUR HIDDEN HOSTILITIES

Nothing is more destructive to a relationship than buried anger. Let's say, for example, that the two of you were fighting a lot before he left, but you didn't know why. Think about it. What was really bothering you? Did you think he didn't make as much money as the sort of man you'd always imagined you'd be with—that he was a bit of a failure? Were you harboring a deep-rooted fury at having been abandoned by your father, who checked out when you were fourteen, and blaming it all on him? Did you resent your husband or lover having a good time when he got together with his friends, feel left out?

Pay attention to any destructive patterns you may have had with men in the past as well. Maybe you tended constantly to compare one man to another, suggesting to whoever was with you that he didn't quite measure up. Maybe you've always been afraid of getting too close to a man because he might hurt or leave you. Maybe you've tried to protect yourself by secretly feeling that no man is good enough for you.

Now is the time to be brutally honest with yourself, and try to uncover just what it is that's causing your hidden hostility. Once you understand the reason, you can *do* something about it. It's a pretty safe bet that if you're feeling any kind of hostility, you'll communicate it to him. Keep reminding yourself that he can't give you what he doesn't have to give—nor can you expect it from him. When you're finally able to say to yourself. "This is the man I love; I'm willing to accept the risks that go along with that, and to accept him as he is," he'll know it, and your relationship will improve dramatically.

LET GO OF YOUR INSECURITIES

What? Let go of the fact that you suffered because your mom was an alcoholic, or because you graduated from high school with only a C average, or feel your breasts are embarrassingly small? That's right. Just give up that kind of thinking. What good has it ever done you? Sure, you may have had problems as a kid— so did most of us. Right, you may not have won a Fulbright, but who among your friend and family has? True, your breasts are smaller than Madonna's—big deal. Putting yourself down because of what's happened to you or how you look is simply not healthy. Once you're able to evaluate yourself realistically, to accept your humanness, which includes weaknesses as well as strengths, you'll communicate that to the man you love, and to everyone else as well. When you are accepting of and secure about yourself, you'll stop making impossible demands (of yourself and others), ease up.

In her lovely book, *Opening Our Hearts to Men*, Susan Jeffers puts it this way: "Our insecurity is, I believe, only our primitive fear of truly leaving our childhood behind and being on our own. We all want the security of being attached to someone else who will save us. But when we cut the chord and see ourselves standing on our own, we get in touch with our own power."

Sally, a forty-one-year-old systems analyst from Albany, New York, told us how this concept worked in her life:

> One morning I woke up and said to myself—as I was brushing my teeth, of all things—*I'm just not going to be insecure anymore*. It was weird—as if the strong part of me was talking to the not-so-strong part of me, and was finally saying, "Enough already! What good had it done me to have totally fallen apart when Harry left? How had it helped me to think every woman in the world was more attractive than I—brighter, better connected, more successful, funnier?" The fact is, during those periods when I was able to be objective, I knew perfectly well that I was as smart and warm and witty as most of the women I knew, but still, I kept on sabotaging myself. Instead of ackowledging that I had a good job, was a caring mother, and had more energy and creativity than practically anybody, I'd always dwell on my weaknesses, and get more and more depressed. But, that morning, something snapped. Putting myself down just didn't make sense anymore. What was the point of going through endless torture, because I wasn't perfect? *Of course* I wasn't perfect. I don't know too many people who are.
>
> I think part of the reason I was so devastated when Harry moved out is that, deep down, I felt he was right; it was inevitable; who would ever want to stay with me? My dad was almost never home. My mother had never seemed to like me much—she was a pretty bitter, rejecting woman (probably because she had felt rejected herself)—so why would anyone else? And then I realized that kind of thinking

was pure craziness. Lots of people had been through worse and come out all right; what was I lugging around all those old insecurities *for*? It was almost as if I had to feel bad about myself to be reminded of who I really was. But, in the bathroom, toothbrush in hand, it occurred to me that the vulnerable little girl I'd been wasn't the woman I'd become. Of course, I'd heard all that stuff before from shrinks, read it in self-help books, but I'd never quite incorporated it. Suddenly, it was right there. How stupid of me not to let go of my insecurities. So I did. Cold turkey. Just by promising myself to stop. And it's worked. Sure, I sometimes start to slip back into a self-destructive pattern, but now, I'm quick to snap out of it. That kind of thinking doesn't do anyone any good—not my husband, nor my kids, nor my friends, and certainly not me. It seems so simple, but it took me a long time to get to this point My marriage improved almost overnight; because I feel so much better about myself, I can help Harry feel better about himself. It's like a little miracle that's happened in our family. What a difference!

NEVER UNDERESTIMATE THE POWER OF AFFECTION

Who doesn't love it—the warm, cozy feeling you get when someone is truly tender and loving? It's so easy to forget the importance of a gentle touch, a quick squeeze of the hand, a little hug, when we're caught up in the business of everyday life. Well, don't. He needs affection, you have the capacity to give it to him, so what are you waiting for? (You need it too, of course, and as with most other good things in life the best way to get what you want you went back is give it—freely.) A phone call mid-morning to tell him you love him, a kiss when you meet after work, a little hug from behind when he's standing at the kitchen counter, putting jam on his toast—there are so many small, loving ways to cheer him up, make him feel good, and we guarantee such gestures will make you feel good, too. So try it. You've got nothing to lose, and a lot of happiness to gain.

LEARN TO SURRENDER TO THE RELATIONSHIP

Hold on now—don't get upset. We're not for a minute suggesting you give yourself up to please him; quite the contrary. We just mean that it's important to get your priorities straight—to accept the fact that this relationship is extremely important to you, and that you may have to make some compromises, or learn to see things a little differently, to keep it healthy.

Karen, a fifty-three-year-old book editor in New York City, describes her experiences with "surrendering."

> Before our separation, Tim used to call me at the office most afternoons just to chat. I'd be frantically busy with some deadline or other, and it really got on my nerves. "What does he *want*?" I use to ask myself. Is he checking on me? Doesn't he have anything better to do with his time? More important, doesn't he realize how valuable my times is? Well, now that we've lived apart and are back together again, everything's different. A colleague pointed out that what Tim may have been doing, in his own sweet way, was flirting with me. I'd never thought of that—what a lovely idea! These days, when he calls, I really concentrate on what he has to say. I realize I just adore this man, and that our relationship is more important than my job—not that I'd like to have to choose between the two, but I'm both touched and flattered that he wants to talk to me. I don't know why I was so bitchy about it before. Now that it's clear he's my number-one priority, it's much easier to give in on the little stuff that used to bother me. I appreciate him more than I ever have, and the feeling seems to be mutual. Sometimes, I even call *him* to chat. I would never, ever have done that before. He loves it!

USE THE SPECIAL THINGS YOU KNOW ABOUT HIM TO MAKE HIM HAPPY

He's crazy about hot cars? Naturally, you can't afford to buy him one of those pricey babies, but you could surprise him with a model Testarossa. He'll get the idea, and love you for it. He's always been a little afraid of heights and you know your annual ski trip to Vale makes him twitchy? Tell him you don't want to go this year—that you'd rather spend the vacation money on a trip to St. Kitts. Acres of soft white sand, emerald green water, and strawberry daiquiris.—*His* kind of thing (pure pleasure for you, too).

You, above all others, know where your man is vulnerable, where he's strong, what he likes, and what he doesn't. So use this precious information to make him happier, more confident. P.S.: Your reward will *not* be in heaven.

TRY TO SEE WHAT'S GOING ON FROM HIS POINT OF VIEW

When we assume that the way we've interpreted what has happened is the *only* way, things can get all out of whack. Of course, your point of view is valid—it's the product of who you are—but other readings are possible. Perhaps your man has been under tremendous pressure at work, so he snaps at you over breakfast. Maybe he's feeling a real financial crunch, so he explodes when he opens the phone bill and sees all those calls you made to your sister. Nobody likes to be snapped or yelled at, nor should you condone such behavior. But at the same time, you have to realize that he has his own set of worries and problems, and the more empathetic and sympathetic you can be about them, the better for both of you.

"The first time he acted annoyed after he came home, my whole body stiffened," says a twenty-nine-year-old executive assistant.

We'd made plans to go to a movie after dinner, and throughout the meal, all I could talk about was how excited I was, and how much fun it was to do things together . . . blah, blah, blah. I was pretty manic. So when Joe suddenly turned to me and said very mildly, but still . . . "Hey, could we eat in peace for minute?" I was totally crushed. I never bothered to think that maybe he was tired, and didn't feel like sitting through three hours of a fast-paced adventure film. I was certain our marriage was over again—kaput. Fini. I threw down my napkin and raced upstairs, sobbing hysterically. When he didn't race right on up after me, I was doubly hysterical.

Later, after I'd finally pulled myself together, I went back downstairs to find him sitting at the table in exactly the same position he'd been in when I left, except that now he had his head in his hands, and was sort of shaking it back and forth. It turned out he'd had possibly one of the worst days of his life at the office—everybody screaming and yelling. Also, he hadn't had time for lunch, and he was starving—but because of the movie, all we'd had for dinner was tuna on pita. Eventually, we wound up laughing over the whole thing, but from that moment on, I promised myself to try to be more sensitive to what was happening with him. He's promised to tell me when something's wrong, too—not easy for a quiet type like Joe, but he's trying.

Another woman we talked to said that when her husband, who'd been back home only a month, asked her how she'd feel if he went deep-sea fishing with his pals for a few days, she went crazy. "I immediately thought: 'he's bored with you; he doesn't love you anymore; he's trying to cut out again,'" Maureen remembers. "But then, after going over the past month in my head, I realized that between worry over cutbacks at work, plus trying to deal with me and the kids in a whole new, more involved way, Ed was probably just plain exhausted, and needed some time off. You've never seen a man look as grateful as he did when I said, 'Absolutely. It's just what you need. Go ahead.'"

LOVE IS THE ANSWER

Love isn't the only element in a happy, well-balanced life, of course, but it sure does help. You've been through a lot to get another chance at the life you want, and now it's important to nurture it. If you keep this clearly in mind—make love your goal—much of the old strife will disappear, and you'll both be more relaxed and fulfilled.

Be a little careful on this one, however. We're not simply talking about your love for him, but also the love you've developed for yourself, the people around you, life itself. It may seem like a paradox, but open yourself up to *all* the opportunities for love in your life, and the love between the two of you will be greatly enriched.

Says Susan Jeffers: "Remember, that if on the last day of our lives we can answer yes to the question, 'Did you warm the world with your love?' we can be at peace with the knowledge that our lives had meaning . . . and that the world is better off for our having been a part of it." Not a bad philosophy, we think, and it wouldn't hurt to remind yourself of it every single day.

COMMIT TO HONESTY

We've talked about this before, but we want to reiterate just how important it is that you both always try to be honest. Only then can you truly let him know how you feel, who you are, what you need. You don't have to overwhelm the man, but you certainly want to be open. And he should be encouraged to do the same. Slowly, as you become more candid with each other, trust will be restored to your relationship. And once the trust is back, you'll be on more solid ground than ever before. Remember, though, that honesty must be tempered with sensitivity and compassion—no cruelty, hostility, negativism. Keep in mind that underneath it all, he's just as needy as you are (or were), and craves your love and support, maybe even more than you crave his.

THINK FUTURE

What do we mean by this? We mean you should make a commitment to the future. The past really *is* past, and now you two have a loving, joyous life ahead of you. Concentrate on that. Plan next summer's vacation. Decide to rent the little cottage in the woods for weekends. Talk about the business you may start together. Plan projects that involve you both. Maybe you used to dream about having a garden the whole neighborhood would envy, but were to lazy to get going on it. *Get going now.* Do all those things you've always secretly been interested in trying, but have, for whatever reasons, put off. Remember the seventies poster that said, "Today is the first day of the rest of your life"? You *are* starting over; you have all things bright and beautiful to look forward to. You've struggled, grown, and now you're ready to take charge of what lies ahead. You can make this relationship anything you want it to be, so love him, laugh with him, delight in him. Starting over can be even more fun than starting out. You know everything you need to know; you're everything you need to be—now just go ahead and enjoy it.

AMERICAN ASSOCIATION FOR MARITAL AND FAMILY THERAPY (National)
1717 K Street NW, 407, Washington D.C. 20006
(202) 452-0109
Description: AAMFT offers referrals to 17,000 professionals (Clinical Members) throughout the country. These are the most qualified therapists associated with AAMFT, and must have either a master's or a Ph.D. in the field. They provide individual counseling and are usually familiar with other resources (clinics and support groups) in their area. Referrals are by zip code and calls must be during business hours.

ACKERMAN INSTITUTE FOR FAMILY THERAPY (New York City)
149 East 78th Street, New York, N.Y. 10021
(212) 879-4900
Description: The Ackerman Institute is a training center that provides referrals for therapists in the New York area. The institute also offers counseling for couples and families. Calls must be made during business hours.

CHRYSALLIS CENTER FOR WOMEN (Minneapolis)
2650 Nicollet Avenue, Minneapolis, Minn. 55408
(612) 871-2603
Description: Chrysallis offers individual counseling, group therapy, and support groups for women. Calls must made be during busi-

ness hours, and the staff cannot give referrals outside of the Minneapolis area. Chrysallis accepts most major insurance towards counseling.

FAMILY AND CHILDREN'S SERVICES (Minnesota)
414 South 8th Street, Minneapolis, Minn. 55404
(612) 340-7494
6900 78th Avenue North, Brooklyn Park, Minn. 55445
(612) 560-4412
9801 DuPont Avenue South, Bloomington, Minn. 55431
(612) 884-7353
Description: This organization offers both individual and group counseling. It does not accept insurance, but has sliding fees based on income. Phone calls are received during business hours and referrals are given for Minnesota only.

FAMILY RESOURCE COALITION (National)
200 South Michigan Avenue Suite 1520, Chicago, Ill. 60604
(312) 341-0900
Description: The Family Resource Coalition offers referrals to numerous "parent support groups" nationwide. Referrals are by telephone, and only during business hours.

FAMILY SERVICE AMERICA (National)
11700 West Lake Park Drive, Milwaukee, Wis. 53224
Description: FSA provides referrals, by mail, to 280 member agencies nationwide. These agencies encompass over 11,000 professionals and generally provide both individual and family counseling.

FAMILY SERVICE OF GREATER BOSTON (Boston)
34 ½ Beacon Street, Boston, Mass. 02108
(617) 523-6400
Description: (Boston affiliate of FSA) This organization offers individual counseling and referrals to local support groups. Most major insurance is accepted. Calls must be made during business hours.

HELP INC. (Philadelphia)
238 South Street, Philadelphia, Pa. 19147
(215) 546-7766
Description: Help offers individual and family counseling and accepts most major insurance. Calls during business hours only.

INSTITUTE OF MARRIAGE AND FAMILY RELATIONS (Virginia)
6116 Rolling Road, Suite 306, Springfield, Va. 22152
(703) 569-2400
Description: The Institute of Marriage and Family Relations offers individual counseling and referrals to professionals in the Virginia area. It does not operate a 24-hour hotline but in an emergency, the answering service will refer calls to a counselor.

JUDEAN SOCIETY (National)
1075 Space Parkway #3316, Mountainview, Calif. 94043
(415) 964-8936
Description: The Judean Society offers individual counseling, support groups and retreats for divorced Catholics (other denominations however, are welcome). Referrals are given to local chapters throughout the country. The society is a volunteer ministry and only accepts donations (all services are free). Calls must be made during business hours.

NATIONAL ORGANIZATION FOR WOMEN (National)
Check local listings for address and telephone numbers of local or state chapter.
Description: NOW gives comprehensive referrals for all services, including counseling, that are available in the area. NOW chapters can only be reached during business hours.

NORTH AMERICAN CONFERENCE OF SEPARATED AND DIVORCED CATHOLICS (National)
1100 South Goodman Street, Rochester, N.Y. 14620
(716) 271-1320
Description: The North American Conference offers referrals to

2,500 peer support groups nationwide. Groups generally have a "Christian flavor" and will put individuals in touch with counselors and other experts in the area. Referrals are only given during business hours.

PARENTS AND CHILDREN'S EQUALITY (National)
5814 Riddle Road, Holidy, Fla. 34690
(813) 938-6911
Description: PACE offers over-the-phone counseling and referrals to professionals throughout the country. It deals primarily with University experts who can assist in divorce proceedings. Operates during business hours.

RESOURCES COUNSELING AND THERAPY CENTER (New York City)
226 East 70th Street, New York, N.Y. 10021
(212) 439-1913
Description: Resources offers individual counseling and support groups. Referrals are given for private therapists in New York area. Resources accepts most major insurance and accepts calls only during business hours.

SOUTHEAST INSTITUTE FOR GROUP AND FAMILY THERAPY (National)
103 Edwards Ridge Road, Chapel Hill, N.C. 27514
(919) 929-1171
Description: The Southeast Institute for Group and Family Therapy provides individual and group counseling and will make referrals to private therapists and clinics nationwide. It accepts most major insurance, and accepts calls only during business hours.

WIVES SELF-HELP FOUNDATION (Philadelphia)
Smylie Times Building Suite 205, 8001 RooseVelt Blvd., Philadelphia, Pa.
(215) 332-2311 (24-hour)
Description: The Wives Self-Help Foundation provides individual,

family and group therapy. It has sliding fees and accepts most major insurance. Phones are answered 24 hours a day.

WOMEN IN TRANSITION (Pennsylvania)
125 South 9th Street, Sheridan Building Suite 502, Philadelphia, Pa. 19107
(215) 922-7500 (24-hour)
Description: Women in Transition provides both group and individual counseling. Referrals are made to therapists throughout Pennsylvania. Women in Transition does not accept insurance. Phones operate 24 hours a day.

BIBLIOGRAPHY

Bakos, Susan Crain. *Dear Superlady of Sex. Men Talk About Their Hidden Desires, Secret Fears, And Number-One Sex Need*. New York: St. Martin's Press, 1990.

————"Secrets of Sensational Sex." *Cosmopolitan*, December 1991, 158–161.

Barbach, Lonnie G. *For Yourself: Fulfillment of Female Sexuality. A Guide to Orgasmic Response*. New York: NAL, 1976

Bushong, Carolyn Nordin. *Loving Him Without Losing You. Eight Steps to Emotional Intimacy Without Addiction*. New York: Continuum, 1991.

Castleman, Michael. *Sexual Solutions: A Guide For Men and the Women Who Love Them*. New York: Touchstone, 1989.

Comfort, Alex. *The Joy of Sex*. New York: Crown, 1986.

Cowan, Connell, and Melvyn Kinder. *Women Men Love. Women Men Leave*. New York: Signet, 1987.

Dyer, Wayne W. *Pulling Your Own Strings. Dynamic Techniques for Dealing with Other People and Mastering Your Own Life*. New York: Avon, 1977.

Feeney, Sheila Anne. "Revenge on the Rebound." *Daily News*, June 27, 1991, 33.

Finzi, Sandra. "*Cosi Fan Tutte*. On the Inevitability of Infidelity." *Family Therapy Networker*, May-June 1989.

Friday, Nancy. *Women on Top. How Real Life Has Changed Women's Sex Fantasies*. New York: Simon & Schuster, 1991.

Fromm, Erich. *The Art of Loving. An Enquiry into the Nature of Love*. New York: Harper & Row, 1956.

Greer-Enders, Deborah. "Why Husbands Don't Leave Their Wives." *Cosmopolitan*, April 1989, 233–35.

Hendrix, Harville. *Getting the Love You Want. A Guide For Couples*. New York: Harper & Row, 1988.

Hite, Shere. *The Hite Report*. New York: Dell, 1987.

Jacoby, Susan. "Self-Esteem: You Can Have It (Almost) All the Time." *Cosmopolitan*, August, 1991 150–53.

Jeffers, Susan. *Opening Our Hearts to Men*. New York: Fawcett Columbine, 1989.

Kingma, Daphne Rose. *Coming Apart. Why Relationships End and How to Live Through the Ending of Yours*. New York: Fawcett Crest, 1987.

Kuriansky, Judy. *How to Love a Nice Guy*. New York: Pocket Books, 1990.

Lane, Cristy, and Laura Ann Stevens. *How to Save Your Troubled Marriage*. New York: St. Martin's Press, 1987.

Lawson, Annette. *Adultry. An Analysis of Love and Betrayal*. New York: Basic Books, 1988.

Marlin, Emily. *Relationships in Recovery. Healing Strategies for Couples and Families*. New York: Harper & Row, 1989.

Medved, Diana. *The Case Against Divorce*. New York: Ivy Books, 1989.

Newman, Mildred, and Bernard Berkowitz, with Jean Owen. *How to Be Your Own Best Friend*. New York: Ballantine, 1971.

Peterson, Karen S. "The Risky Business of Adultery." *USA Today*. Section D, July 16, 1990, 1–2.

Pittman, Frank. *Private Lies: Infidelity and the Betrayal of Intimacy*. New York: W. W. Norton, 1989.

————"Mending Broken Ties." *New Woman*, November 1990, 41–43.

Rice, Rebecca. "First You Separate, Then You Reconcile—Or Do You?" *Cosmopolitan*. March 1992, p. 82.

Seligman, Martin. *Learned Optimism: The Skill to Conquer Life's Obstacles*. New York: Random House, 1991.

Stein, Ben. "A Married Man Warns Single Girls Away." *Cosmopolitan*, March 1991, 174–76.

Steinem, Gloria. *Revolution From Within*. New York: Little, Brown, 1991.

232 • *Diane Baroni and Betty Kelly*

Spock, Benjamin. *Dr. Spock's Baby & Child Care*. New York: Pocket Books, 1981.

Trafford, Abigail. *Crazy Time*. New York: Harper & Row, 1982.

Vatsyayana. *Art of Love, The Second Book of Kama Sutra*. New York: Medical Press of New York, 1962.

Vaughan, Diane. *Uncoupling. How Relationships Come Apart*. New York: Vintage, 1987.

Vaughan, Peggy. *The Monogamy Myth. A New Understanding of Affairs and How to Survive Them*. New York: Newmarket Press, 1989.

Wanderer, Zev, and Tracy Cabot. *Letting Go. A Twelve-Week Personal Action Program to Overcome a Broken Heart*. New York: Dell, 1978.

Winokur, Jon. *Friendly Advice*. New York: Dutton, 1990.

Zilbergeld, Bernie. *Male Sexuality*. New York: Bantam, 1978.

Zola, Marion. *All the Good Ones Are Married*. New York: Times Books, 1981.